SELF INVESTMENT

ORISON SWETT MARDEN

CONTENTS

1

IF YOU CAN TALK WELL

A good conversationalist is one who has ideas, who reads, thinks, listens, and who has therefore something to says Sir WALTER SCOTT.

WHEN Charles W. Eliot was president of Harvard, he said, "I recognize but one mental acquisition as an essential part of the education of a lady or gentleman, namely, an accurate and refined use of the mother-tongue."

There is no other one thing which enables us to make so good an impression, especially upon those who do not know us thoroughly, as the ability to converse well.

To be a good conversationalist, able to interest people, to rivet their attention, to draw them to you naturally, by the very superiority of your conversational ability, is to be the possessor of a very great accomplishment, one which is superior to all others. It not only helps you to make a good impression upon strangers, it also helps you to make and keep friends. It opens doors and softens hearts. It makes you interesting in all sorts of company. It helps you to get on in the world. It sends you clients, patients, customers. It helps you into the best society, even though you are poor.

A man who can talk well, who has the art of putting things in an attractive way, who can interest others immediately by his power of speech, has a very great advantage over one who may know more than he, but who cannot express himself with ease or eloquence.

No matter how expert you may be in any other art or accomplishment, you cannot use your expertness always and everywhere as you can the power to converse well. If you are a musician, no matter how talented you may be, or how many years you may have spent in perfecting yourself in your specialty, or how much it may have cost you, only comparatively few people can ever hear or appreciate your music.

You may be a fine singer, and yet travel around the world without having an opportunity of showing your accomplishment, or without anyone guessing your specialty. But wherever you go and in whatever society you are, no matter what your station in life may be, you talk.

You may be a painter, you may have spent years with great masters, and yet, unless you have very marked ability so that your pictures are hung in the *salons* or in the great art galleries, comparatively few people will ever see them. But if you are an artist in conversation, everyone who comes in contact with you will see your life-picture, which you have been painting ever since you began to talk. Everyone knows whether you are an artist or a bungler.

In fact, you may have a great many accomplishments which people occasionally see or enjoy, and you may have a very beautiful home and a lot of property which comparatively few people ever know about; but if you are a good converser, everyone with whom you talk will feel the influence of your skill and charm.

A noted society leader, who has been very successful in the launching of *debutantes* in society, always gives this advice to her *protégés,* "Talk, talk. It does not matter much what you say, but chatter away lightly and gaily. Nothing embarrasses and bores the average man so much as a girl who has to be entertained."

There is a helpful suggestion in this advice. The way to learn to talk is to talk. The temptation for people who are unaccustomed to society, and who feel diffident, is to say nothing themselves and listen to what others say.

Good talkers are always sought after in society. Everybody wants to invite Mrs. Soami-So to dinners or receptions because she is such a good talker. She entertains. She may have many defects, but people enjoy her society because she can talk well.

Conversation, if used as an educator, is a tremendous power developer; but talking without thinking, without an effort to express oneself with clearness, conciseness, or efficiency, mere chattering, or gossiping, the average society small talk, will never get hold of the best thing in a man. It lies too deep for such superficial effort.

Thousands of young people who envy such of their mates as are getting on faster than they are keep on wasting their precious evenings and their half-holidays,· saying nothing but the most frivolous, frothy, senseless things, things which do not rise to the level of humor, but the foolish, silly talk which demoralizes one's ambition, lowers one's ideals and all the standards of life, because it begets habits of superficial and senseless thinking. On the streets, on the cars, and in public places, loud, coarse voices are heard in light, flippant, slipshod speech, in coarse slang expression.

"You're talking through your hat"; "Search me"; " You just bet"; " Well, that's the limit"; "I hate that man; he gets on my nerves," and a score of other such vulgarities we often hear.

Nothing else will indicate your fineness or coarseness of culture, your breeding or lack of it, so quickly as your conversation. It will tell your whole life's story. What you say, and how you say it, will betray all your secrets, will give the world your true measure.

There is no other accomplishment or acquirement which you can use so constantly and effectively, which will give so much pleasure to your friends, as fine conversation. There is no doubt that the gift of language was intended to be a much greater accomplishment than the majority of us have ever made of it.

Most of us are bunglers in our conversation, because we do not make an art of it; we do not take the trouble or pains to learn to talk well. We do not read enough or think enough. Most of us express ourselves in sloppy, slipshod English, because it is so much easier to do so ·than it is to think before we speak, to make an effort to express ourselves with elegance, ease, and power.

Poor conversers excuse themselves for not trying to improve by saying that "good talkers are born, not made." We might as well say that good lawyers, good physicians, or good merchants are born, not made. None of them would ever get very far without hard work. This is the price of all achievement that is of value.

Many a man owes his advancement very largely to his ability to converse well. The ability to interest people in your conversation, to hold them, is a great power. The man who bungles in his expression, who knows a thing, but never can put it in logical, interesting, or commanding language, is always placed at a great disadvantage.

I know a business man who has cultivated the art of conversation to such an extent that it is a great treat to listen to him. His language flows with such liquid, limpid beauty, his words are chosen with such exquisite delicacy, taste, and accuracy, there is such a refinement in his diction that he charms everyone who hears him speak. All his life he has been a reader of the finest prose and poetry, and has cultivated conversation as a fine art.

You may think you are poor and have no chance in life. You may be situated so that others are dependent upon you, and you may not be able to go to school or college, or to study music or art, as you long to; you may be tied down to an iron environment; you may be tortured with an unsatisfied, disappointed ambition; and yet you can become an interesting talker, because in every sentence you utter you can practise the best form of expression. Every book you read, every person with whom you converse, who uses good English, can help you.

Few people think very much' about how they are going to express themselves. They use the first words that come to them. They do not think of forming a sentence so that it will have beauty, brevity, transparency, power. The words flow from their lips helter-skelter, with little thought of arrangement or order.

Now and then we meet a real artist in conversation, and it is such a treat and delight that we wonder why the most of us should be such bunglers in our conversation, that we should make such a botch of the medium of communication between human beings, when it is capable of being made the art of arts.

I have met a dozen persons in my lifetime who have given me such a glimpse of its superb possibilities that it has made all other arts seem comparatively unimportant to me.

I was once a visitor at Wendell Phillips's home in Boston, and the music of his voice, the liquid charm of his words, the purity, the transparency of his diction, the profundity of his knowledge, the fascination of his personality, and his marvelous art of putting things, I shall never forget. He sat down on the sofa beside me and talked as he would to an old schoolmate, and it seemed to me that I had never before heard such exquisite English.

I have met several English people who possessed that marvelous power of " soul in conversation which charms all who come under its spell."

Mrs. Mary A. Livermore, Julia Ward Howe, and Elizabeth Stuart Phelps Ward had this wonderful conversational charm, as has ex-President Eliot of Harvard.

The quality of the conversation is everything. We all know people who use the choicest language and express their thoughts in fluent, liquid diction, who impress us by the wonderful flow of their conversation; but that is all there is to it. They do not impress us with their thoughts; they do not stimulate us to action. We do not feel any more determined to do something in the world, to be somebody, after we have heard them talk than we felt before.

We know other people who talk very little, but whose words are so full of meat and stimulating brain force that we feel ourselves multiplied many times by the power they have injected into us.

In olden times the art of conversation reached a much higher standard than that of to-day. The deterioration is due to the complete revolution in the conditions of modern civilization. Formerly people had almost no other way of communicating their thoughts than by speech. Knowledge of all kinds was disseminated almost wholly through the spoken word. There were no great daily newspapers, no magazines or periodicals of any kind.

The great discoveries of vast wealth in the precious minerals, the new world opened up by inventions and discoveries, and the great impetus to ambition have changed all this. In this lightning-express age., in these strenuous times, when everybody has the mania to attain wealth and position, we no longer have time to reflect with deliberation, and to develop our powers of conversation. In these great news-paper and periodical days, when everybody can get for one or a few cents the news and information which it has cost thousands of dollars to collect, everybody sits behind the morning sheet or is buried in a book or magazine. There is no longer the same need of communicating thought by the spoken word, as there was formerly.

Oratory is becoming a lost art for the same reason. Printing has become so cheap that even the poorest homes can get more reading for a few dollars than kings and noblemen could afford in the Middle Ages.

It is a rare thing to find a polished conversationalist to-day. So rare is it to hear one speaking exquisite English, and using a superb diction, that it is indeed a luxury.

Good reading, however, will not only broaden the mind and give new ideas, but it will also increase one's vocabulary, and that is a great aid to conversation. Many people have good thoughts and ideas, but they cannot express them because of the poverty of their vocabulary. They have not words enough to clothe their ideas and make them attractive. They talk around in a circle, repeat and repeat, because, when they want a particular word to convey their exact meaning, they cannot find it.

If you are ambitious to talk well, you must be as much as possible in the society of well-bred, cultured people. If you seclude yourself, though you are a college graduate, you will be a poor converser.

We all sympathize with people, especially the timid and shy, who have that awful feeling of repression and stifling of thought, when they make an effort to say something and cannot. Timid young people often suffer keenly in this way in attempting to declaim at school or college. But many a great orator went through the same sort of experience when he first attempted to speak in public, and was often deeply humiliated by his blunders and failures. There is no other way, however, to become an orator or a good conversationalist than by constantly trying to express oneself efficiently and elegantly.

If you find that your ideas fly from you when you attempt to express them, that you stammer and flounder about for words which you are unable to find, you may be sure that every honest effort you make, even if you fail in your attempt, will make it all the easier for you to speak well the next time. It is remarkable, if one keeps on .trying, how quickly he will conquer his awkwardness and self-consciousness, and will gain ease of manner and facility of expression.

Everywhere we see people placed at a tremendous disadvantage because they have never learned the art of putting their ideas into interesting, telling language. We see brainy men at public gatherings, when momentous questions are being discussed, sit silent, unable to tell what they know, when they are infinitely better informed than those who are making a great deal of display of oratory or smooth talk.

People with a lot of ability, who know a great deal, often appear like a set of dummies in company, while some superficial, shallow brained person holds the attention of those present simply because he can tell what he knows in an interesting way. They are constantly humiliated and embarrassed when away from those who happen to know their real worth, because they cannot carry on an intelligent conversation upon any topic. There are hundreds of these silent people at our national capital many of them wives of husbands who have suddenly and unexpectedly come into political prominence.

Many people and this is especially true of scholars seem to think that the great *desideratum* in life is to get as much valuable information into the head as possible. But it is just as important to know how to give out knowledge in a palatable manner as to acquire it. You may be a profound scholar, you may be well read in history and in politics, you may be wonderfully well-posted in science, literature, and art, and yet, if your knowledge is locked up within you, you will always be placed at a great disadvantage.

Locked-up ability may give the individual some satisfaction, but it must be exhibited, expressed in some attractive way, before the world will appreciate it or give credit for it. It does not matter how valuable the rough diamond may be, no explaining, no describing its marvels of beauty within, and its great value, would avail; nobody would appreciate it until it was ground and polished and the light let into its depths to reveal its hidden brilliancy. Conversation is to the man what the cutting of the diamond is to the stone. The grinding does riot add anything to the diamond. It merely reveals its wealth.

How little parents realize the harm they are doing their children by allowing them to grow up ignorant of or indifferent to the marvelous possibilities in the art of conversation. In the majority of homes, children are allowed to mangle the English language in a most painful way.

Nothing else will develop the brain and character more than the constant effort to talk well, intelligently, interestingly, upon all sorts of topics. There is a splendid discipline in the constant effort to express one's thoughts in clear language and in an interesting manner. We know people who are such superb conversers that no one would ever dream that they have not had the advantages of the higher schools.

Many a college graduate has been silenced and put to shame by people who have never even been to a high school, but who have cultivated the art of self-expression.

The school and the college employ the student comparatively a few hours a day for a few years; conversation is a training in a perpetual school. Many get the best part of their education in this school.

Conversation is a great ability discoverer, a great revealer of possibilities and resources. It stimulates thought wonderfully. We think more of ourselves if we can talk well, if we can interest and hold others. The power to do so increases our self-respect, our self-confidence.

No man knows what he really possesses until he makes his best effort to express to others what is in him. Then the avenues of the mind fly open, the faculties are on the alert. Every good converser has felt a power come to him from the listener which he never felt before, and which often stimulates and inspires to fresh endeavor. The mingling of thought with thought, the contact of mind with mind, develops new powers, as the mixing of two chemicals produces a new third substance.

To converse well one must listen well also.

This means one must hold oneself in a receptive attitude.

We are not only poor conversationalists, but we are poor listeners as well. We are too impatient to listen. Instead of being attentive and eager to drink in the story or the information, we have not enough respect for the talker to keep quiet. We look about impatiently, perhaps snap our watch, play a tattoo with our fingers on a chair or a table, hitch about as if we were bored and were anxious to get away, and interrupt the speaker before he reaches his conclusion. In fact, we are such an impatient people that we have no time for anything except to push ahead, to elbow our way through the crowd to get the position or the money we desire. Our life is feverish and unnatural. We have no time to develop charm of manner, or elegance of diction. "We are too intense for epigram or repartee. We lack time."

Nervous impatience is a conspicuous characteristic of the American people. Everything bores us which does not bring us more business or more money, or which does not help us to attain the position for which we are striving. Instead of enjoying our friends, we are inclined to look upon them as so many rungs in a ladder, and to value them in proportion as they furnish readers for our books, send us patients, clients, customers, or show their ability to give us a boost for a coveted position.

Before these days of hurry and drive, before this age of excitement, it was considered one of the greatest luxuries possible to be a listener in a group surrounding an intelligent talker. It was better than most modern lectures, than anything one could find in a book; for there was a touch of personality, a charm of style, a magnetism which held, a superb personality which fascinated. For the hungry soul yearning for an education, to drink in knowledge from those wise lips was to be fed with a royal feast indeed.

But to-day everything is "touch and go." We have no time to stop on the street and give a decent salutation. It is: "How do?" or "Morning," accompanied by a sharp nod of the head, instead of a graceful bow. We have no time for the graces and the charms. Everything must give way to the material.

We have no time for the development of a fine manner; the charm of the days of chivalry and leisure has almost vanished from our civilization. A new type of individual has sprung up. We work like Trojans during the day, and then rush to a theater or other place of amusement in the evening. Vie have no time to make our own amusement or to develop the faculty of humor and fun-making as people used to do. We pay people for doing that while we sit and laugh. We are like some college boys, who depend upon tutors to carry them through their examinations they expect to buy their education ready-made.

Life is becoming so artificial, so forced, so diverse from naturalness, we drive our human engines at such a fearful speed, that our finer life is crushed out. Spontaneity and humor, and the possibility of a fine culture and · a superb charm of personality in us are almost impossible and extremely rare.

One cause for our conversational decline is a lack of sympathy. We are too selfish, too busily engaged in our own welfare, and wrapped up in our own little world, too intent upon our own self-promotion to be interested in others. No one can make a good converser who is not sympathetic. You must be able to enter into another's life, to live it with the other person, in order to be a good talker or a good listener.

Walter Besant used to tell of a clever woman who had a great reputation as a conversationalist, though she talked very little. She had such a cordial, sympathetic manner that she helped the timid and the shy to say their best things, and made them feel at home. She dissipated their fears, and they could say things to her which they could not say to anyone else. People thought her an interesting conversationalist because she had this ability to call out the best in others.

If you would make yourself agreeable you must be able to enter into the life of the people with whom you converse, and you must touch them along the lines of their interest. No matter how much you may know about a subject, if it does not happen to interest those to whom you are talking your efforts will be largely lost.

It is pitiable, sometimes, to see men standing around at the average reception or club gathering, dumb, almost helpless, and powerless to enter heartily into the conversation because they are in a subjective mood. They are thinking, thinking; thinking business, business, business; thinking how they can get on a little faster get more business, more clients, more patients, or more readers for their books, or a better house to live in; how they can make more show. They do not enter heartily into the lives of others, or abandon themselves to the occasion enough to make good talkers. They are cold and reserved, distant, because their minds are somewhere else, their affections on themselves and their own affairs. There are only two things that interest them, business and their own little world. If you talk about these things, they are interested at once; but they do not care a snap about your affairs, how you get on, or what your ambition is, or how they can help you. Our conversation will never reach a high standard while we live in such a feverish, selfish, and unsympathetic state.

Great conversationalists have always been very tactful interesting without offending. It does not do to stab people if you would interest them, nor to drag out their family skeletons. Some people have the peculiar quality of touching the best that is in us; others stir up the bad. Every time they come into our presence they irritate us. Others allay all that is disagreeable." They never touch our sensitive spots, sore spots, and they call out all that is spontaneous and sweet and beautiful.

Lincoln was master of the art of making himself interesting to everybody he met. He put people at ease with his stories and jokes, and made them feel so completely at home in his presence that they opened up their mental treasures to him without reserve. Strangers were always glad to talk with him, because he was so cordial and quaint, and always gave more than he got.

A sense of humor such as Lincoln had is, of course, a great addition to one's conversational powers. But not everyone can be funny; and, if you lack the sense of humor, you will make yourself ludicrous by attempting to be so.

A good conversationalist, however, is not too serious. He does not deal too much with facts, no matter how important. Facts, statistics, weary. Vivacity is absolutely necessary. Heavy conversation bores; too light, disgusts.

Therefore, to be a good conversationalist you must be spontaneous, buoyant, natural, sympathetic, and must show a spirit of good will .. You must feel a spirit of helpfulness, and must enter heart and soul into things which interest others. You must get the attention of people and hold it by interesting them, and you can only interest them by a warm sympathy a real friendly sympathy. If you are cold, distant, and unsympathetic you cannot hold their attention.

You must be broad, tolerant. A narrow, stingy soul never talks well. A man who is always violating your sense of taste, of justice, and of fairness, never interests you. You lock tight all the approaches to your inner self, every avenue is closed to him. Your magnetism and your helpfulness are thus cut off, and the conversation is perfunctory, mechanical, and without life or feeling.

You must bring your listener close to you, must open your heart wide, and exhibit a broad, free nature, and an open mind. You must be responsive, so that he will throw wide open every avenue of his nature and give you free access to his heart of hearts. .

If a man is a success anywhere, it ought to be in his personality, in his power to express himself in strong, effective, interesting language. He should not be obliged to give a stranger an inventory of his possessions in order to show that he has achieved something. A greater wealth should flow from his lips, and express itself in his manner.

No amount of natural ability or education or good clothes, no amount of money, will make you appear well if you cannot express yourself in good language.

2
PUT BEAUTY INTO YOUR LIFE

"Beauty is God's handwriting."

There is no beautifier of complexion, or form, or behavior, like the wish to scatter joy, and not pain, around us. Emerson.

WHEN the barbarians overran Greece, desecrated her temples, and destroyed her beautiful works of art, even their savageness was somewhat tamed by the sense of beauty which prevailed everywhere. They broke her beautiful statues, it is true; but the spirit of beauty refused to die, and it transformed the savage heart and awakened even in the barbarian a new power. From the apparent death of Grecian art Roman art was born. "Cyclops forging iron for Vulcan could not stand against Pericles forging thought for Greece." The barbarian's club which destroyed the Grecian statues was no match for the chisel of Phidias and Praxiteles.

There was no art in Italy until the Romans conquered Greece and carried her art treasures back to Rome. It was the famous "Horse's Head," the "Farnese Bull," the "Marble Faun," the "Dying Gladiator," the "Boy Taking a Thorn From His Foot" that were practically the basis of the whole wonderful Italian art. These, aided by the marvelous Italian marbles, were the first to arouse the slumbering artistic faculties in the Italian people.

"What is the best education?" someone asked Plato, many centuries ago. "It is," he replied, "that which gives to the body and to the soul all the beauty and all the perfection of which they are capable."

The life that would be complete; that would be sweet and sane, as well as strong, must be softened and enriched by a love of the beautiful.

A man is a very broad, omnivorous animal, and his harmonious development demands a great variety of food, both mental and physical. No matter what element we omit in his bill of fare, there is a corresponding loss, omission, or weakness in his life. You cannot get a full, complete man on half a bill of fare. You cannot nourish his body and starve his soul, and expect him to be symmetrical, well . balanced, poised; nor can you starve his body and nourish his soul, and expect him to be a giant on the physical as well as on the spiritual plane.

When children do not get a sufficient or proper variety of food, when they are deprived of any element necessary for the nourishment of brain, nerve, or muscle, there is a corresponding lack in their development. For want of a properly balanced diet they grow up lopsided, unbalanced, and unsymmetrical.

If, for instance, a child does not get enough phosphate of lime in his food, Nature cannot build strong, firm bone; the framework of the body is weak, the bones are soft, and the child is liable to have" rickets." If his diet is lacking in nitrogenous or muscle-making material, his muscles will be weak and flabby, he will never have "the wrestling thews that throw the world." If the phosphatic elements, the builders of brain and nerves, be deficient, his whole organism will suffer, brain and nerves will be incomplete, lacking in energy, undeveloped, just as the body of a growing child requires a wide variety of physical food to make him strong, beautiful, and healthy, so man requires many kinds of mental food to nourish his mind and make it grow strong, active, and healthy.

The marvelous material resources of our country have so stimulated the national ambition for wealth that we are in danger of overdeveloping the material faculties at the expense of the higher and finer ones.

It is not enough for us to cultivate mere physical and intellectual strength. If the esthetic side of one's being an appreciation of all that is beautiful in nature and art is not fostered, the life will be like a country without flowers or birds, sweet scents or sounds, color or music. It may be strong, but it will lack the graces that would adorn its strength and make it attractive.

The Creator has not covered the world with loveliness, filled it with music, and spread the beauties of earth and sea on every hand for nothing. Man is the explanation of this lavishness of beauty.

If you would be a man in the larger sense of the word, you must not be content to make one small clearing in the forest of your nature and let all the rest remain unreclaimed. The pursuit of merchandise, of material gain in any form, develops only a very small part of one's being, and that often the selfish and coarser side.

There is a lack in the make-up of a person who has no appreciation of beauty; who does not thrill before a great picture or an entrancing sunset, or a glimpse of beauty in nature.

Savages have no appreciation of beauty. They have a passion for adornment, but there is nothing to show that their esthetic faculties are developed. They merely obey their animal instincts and passions.

But as civilization advances ambition grows, wants multiply, and higher and higher faculties show themselves, until in the highest expression of civilization, we find aspiration and love of the beautiful most highly developed. We find it manifested on the person, in the home, in the environment.

The late Professor Charles Eliot Norton of Harvard University, one of the finest thinkers of his day, said that beauty has played an immense part in the development of the highest qualities in human beings; and that civilization could be measured by its architecture, sculpture, and painting.

A love for the beautiful has a refining, softening, enriching influence upon character which nothing else can supply. It is most unfortunate for a child to be brought up in an atmosphere in which it is missing, and where only a money-loving spirit is manifested, where he is trained to think that the most important thing in life is to get more money, more houses and lands, instead of more manhood, more nobility, more sweetness, more beauty.

It is cruel to twist a young life out of its God-intended orbit by such false training, to wrench it from its spiritual center and set it toward a material goal, while the mind is plastic and capable of being molded to any impression, good or evil.

Children should live in the midst of beauty, in art and nature, as much as possible. No opportunity to call their attention to a beautiful object should be lost. In this way their whole lives may be enriched by treasures which no amount of money in after years can purchase for them.

What an infinite satisfaction comes from beginning early in life to cultivate our finer qualities, to develop higher sentiments, purer tastes, and more delicate feelings, the love of the beautiful in all its varied forms of expression!

One can make no better investment than the cultivation of a taste for the beautiful, for it will bring rainbow hues and enduring joys to the whole life. It will not only greatly increase one's capacity for happiness, but also one's efficiency.

A remarkable instance of the elevating, refining influence of beauty has been demonstrated by a Chicago school-teacher, who fitted up in her school a "beauty corner" for her pupils.

It was furnished with a stained glass window, a divan covered with an Oriental rug, and a few fine photographs and paintings, among which was a picture of the Sistine Madonna. Several other esthetic trifles, artistically arranged, completed the furnishings of the" beauty corner." The children took great delight in their little retreat, especially in the exquisite coloring of the stained glass window. Insensibly their conduct and demeanor were affected by the beautiful objects with which they daily associated. They became more gentle, more refined, more thoughtful and considerate.

A young Italian boy, in particular, who had been incorrigible before the establishment of the "beauty corner," became, in a short time, so changed and softened that the teacher was astonished. One day she asked what it was that had recently made him so good. Pointing to the picture of the Sistine Madonna the boy said, "How can a feller do bad things when she's looking at him?"

Character is fed largely through the eye and ear. The thousand voices in nature of bird and insect and brook, the soughing of the wind through the trees, the scent of flower and meadow, the myriad tints in earth and sky, in ocean and forest, mountain and hill, are just as important for the

15

development of a real man as the education he receives in the schools. If you take no beauty into your life through the eye or the ear to stimulate and develop your esthetic faculties, your nature will be hard, juiceless, and unattractive.

Nothing else can ever quite take the place in life of the development of the faculty for appreciating the beautiful. It is a connecting link between man and the Great Author of the beautiful. At no other time do our spirits come into such close touch with the divine as when we are lost in the contemplation of the sublimity, the grandeur and perfection of the universe. Then we actually seem to see the creative processes of the Infinite Mind.

Just try the effect of putting beauty into your life, a little every day. You will find it magical. It will broaden and light up your outlook upon the world as the acquisition of money or fame never can. Put variety into your mental bill of fare as well as into your physical. It will pay you rich returns. No matter if you are strong and rugged and able to work every day in the year, your mind needs a change even if your body does not. Vacation is as much a necessity from a character as from a health point of view. If you feed upon the same mental food, if you have practically the same experiences every day of the three hundred and sixty-five, year in and year out, there will be disaster somewhere in your life.

Unfoldment of the esthetic faculties is one of the most important factors in our success and happiness, in the ennobling and uplifting of our lives. Ruskin's love of the beautiful gave his whole life an indescribable charm and loftiness. It kept him looking upward as well as outward. It purified and exalted, while it held him spellbound. It was the constant reaching out after the beautiful in nature and art, in his divine interpretation of all that man and nature mean which gave zest and enthusiasm, earnestness and divine significance to his great life-work.

Beauty is a quality of Divinity, and to live much with the beautiful is to live close to the Divine. "The more we see of beauty everywhere; in nature, in life, in man and child, in work and rest, in the outward and the inward world, the more we see of God (good)."

There are many evidences in the New Testament that Christ was a great lover of the beautiful, especially in nature. Was it not He who said: "Consider the lilies of the field; they toil not, neither do they spin; yet Solomon in all his glory was not arrayed like one of these"?

Back of the lily and the rose, back of the landscape, back of all beautiful things that enchant us, there is the great Lover of the beautiful and great beauty Principle. Every star that twinkles in the sky, every flower, bids us look behind it for its source, points us to the great Author of the beautiful.

The love of beauty plays a very important part in the poised, symmetrical life. We little realize how much we are influenced by beautiful people and things. We may see them so often that they become common in our experience and fail to attract much of our conscious attention, but every beautiful picture, every beautiful sunset and bit of landscape, every beautiful face and form and flower beauty in any form, wherever we encounter it ennobles, refines. and elevates character.

There is everything in keeping the soul and mind responsive to beauty. It is a great refreshener, recuperator, life-giver, health promoter.

Our American life tends to kill the finer sentiments; to discourage the development of charm and grace as well as beauty; it overemphasizes the value of material things and under-estimates that of esthetic things, which are far more developed in countries where the dollar is not the God.

As long as we persist in sending all the sap and energy of our being into the moneymaking gland or faculty and letting the social faculty, the esthetic faculty, and all the finer, nobler faculties lie dormant, and even die, we certainly cannot expect a well-rounded and symmetrical life, for only faculties that are used, brain cells that are exercised, grow; all others atrophy. If the finer instincts in man and the nobler qualities that live in the higher brain are under-developed, and the coarser instincts which dwell in the lower brain close to the brute faculties are overdeveloped, man must pay the penalty of animality and will lack appreciation of all that is finest and most beautiful in life.

Isn't it pitiable, shameful, almost criminal that we give practically all our efforts to the useful, and allow the beautiful to play such an unimportant part in our life; that we should take so little pains to read God's handwriting in every created thing?

"The vision that you hold in your mind, the ideal that is enthroned in your heart, this you will build your life by, this you will become." It is the quality of mind, of ideals, and not mere things, that make a man.

It is as essential to cultivate the esthetic faculties and the heart qualities as to cultivate what we call the intellect. The time will come when our children will be taught, both at home and in school, to consider beauty as a most precious gift, which must be preserved in purity, sweetness, and cleanliness, and regarded as a divine instrument of education.

There is no investment which will give such returns as the culture of the finer self, the development of the sense of the beautiful, the sublime, and the true; the development of qualities that are crushed out or strangled in the mere dollar-chaser.

There are a thousand evidences in us that we were intended for temples of beauty, of sweetness, of loveliness, of beautiful ideas, and not mere storehouses for vulgar things.

There is nothing else which will pay so well as to train the finest and truest, the most beautiful qualities in us in order that we may see beauty everywhere and be able to extract sweetness from everything.

Everywhere we go there are a thousand things to educate the best there is in us. Every sunset, landscape, mountain, hill, and tree has secrets of charm and beauty waiting for us. In every patch of meadow or wheat, in every leaf and flower, the trained eye will see beauty which would charm an angel. The cultured ear will find harmony in forest and field, melody in the babbling brook, and untold pleasure in all Nature's songs.

Whatever our vocation, we should resolve that we will not strangle all that is finest and noblest in us for the sake of the dollar, but that we will *put beauty into our life at every opportunity.*

Just in proportion to your love for the beautiful will you acquire its charms and develop its graces. The beauty thought, the beauty ideal, will outpicture themselves in the face and manner. If you are in love with beauty you will be an artist of some kind. Your profession may be to make the home beautiful and sweet, or you may work at a trade; but whatever your vocation, if you are In love with the beautiful, it will purify your taste, elevate and enrich your life, and make you a true artist instead of a mere artisan.

There is no doubt that in the future beauty will play an infinitely greater part in civilized life than it has thus far. It is becoming commercialized everywhere. The trouble with us is that the tremendous material prizes in this land of opportunity are so tempting that we have lost sight of the higher man. We have developed ourselves along the animal side of our nature; the greedy, grasping side, The great majority of us are still living in the basement of our beings. Now and then one ascends to the upper stories and gets a glimpse of the life beautiful, the life worthwhile.

There is nothing on earth that will so slake the thirst of the soul as the beauty which ex presses itself in sweetness and light.

An old traveling man relates that once when on a trip to the West he sat next to an elderly lady who every now and then would lean out of the open window and pour some thick salt it seemed to him from a bottle. When she had emptied the bottle she would refill it from a hand-bag.

A friend to whom this man related the incident told him he was acquainted with the lady, who was a great lover of flowers and an earnest follower of the precept: " Scatter your flowers as you go, for you may never travel the same road again." He said she added greatly to the beauty of the landscape along the railroads on which she traveled, by her custom of scattering flower seeds along the track as she rode. Many roads have thus been beautified and refreshed by this old lady's love of the beautiful and her effort to scatter beauty wherever she went.

If we would all cultivate a love of the beautiful and scatter beauty seeds as we go through life, what a paradise this earth would become!

What a splendid opportunity a vacation in the country offers to put beauty into the life; to cultivate the esthetic faculties, which in most people are wholly undeveloped and inactive! To some it is like going into God's great gallery of charm and beauty. They find in the landscape, the valley, the mountains, the fields, the meadows, the flowers, the streams, the brooks and the rivers, riches that no money can buy; beauties that would enchant the angels. But this beauty and glory cannot be bought; they are only for those who can see them, appreciate them who can read their message and respond to their affinity.

Have you ever felt the marvelous power of beauty in nature? If not, you have missed one of the most exquisite joys in life. I was once going through the Yosemite Valley, and after riding one hundred miles in a stagecoach over rough mountain roads, I was so completely exhausted that it did not seem as though I could keep my seat until we traveled over the ten more miles which would bring us to our destination. But on looking down from the top of the mountain I caught a glimpse of the celebrated Yosemite Falls and the surrounding scenery, just as the sun broke through the clouds; and there was revealed a picture of such rare beauty and marvelous picturesqueness that every particle of fatigue, brain-fag, and muscle weariness departed in an instant. My whole soul thrilled with a winged sense of sublimity, grandeur, and beauty, which I had never before experienced, and which I never can forget. I felt a spiritual uplift which brought tears of joy to my eyes.

No one can contemplate the wonderful beauties of Nature and doubt that the Creator must have intended that man, made in His own image and likeness, should be equally beautiful.

Beauty of character, charm of manner, attractiveness and graciousness of expression, a godlike bearing, are our birthrights. Yet how ugly, stiff, coarse, and harsh in appearance and bearing many of us are! No one can afford to disregard his good looks or personal appearance.

But if we wish to beautify the outer, we must first beautify the inner, for every thought and every motion shapes the delicate tracings of our face for ugliness or beauty. Inharmonious and destructive attitudes of mind will warp and mar the most beautiful features.

Shakespeare says: "God has given you one face and you make yourselves another." The mind can make beauty or ugliness at will.

A sweet, noble disposition is absolutely essential to the highest form of beauty. It has transformed many a plain face. A bad temper, ill nature, jealousy, will ruin the most beautiful face ever created. After all, there is no beauty like that produced by a lovely character. N either cosmetics, massage, nor drugs can remove the lines of prejudice, selfishness, envy, anxiety, mental vacillation that are the results of wrong thought habits.

Beauty is from within. If every human being would cultivate a gracious mentality, not only would what he expressed be artistically beautiful, but also his body. There would indeed be grace and charm, a superiority about him, which would be even greater than mere physical beauty.

We have all seen even very plain women who because of the charm of their personality impressed us as transcendently beautiful. The exquisite soul qualities expressed through the body transformed it into their likeness. A fine spirit speaking through the plainest body will make it beautiful.

Someo ne, speaking of Fanny Kemble, said: "Although she was very stout and short, and had a very red face, yet she impressed me as the supreme embodiment of majestic attributes. I never saw so commanding a personality in feminine form. Any type of mere physical beauty would have paled to insignificance by her side."

Antoine Berryer says truly: "There are no ugly women. There are only women who do not know how to look pretty."

The highest beauty; beauty that is far superior to mere regularity of feature or form is within reach of everybody. It is perfectly possible for one, even with the homeliest face, to make herself beautiful by the habit of perpetually holding in mind the beauty thought not the thought of mere superficial beauty, but that of heart beauty, soul beauty, and by the cultivation of a spirit of kind ness, hopefulness, and unselfishness.

The basis of all real personal beauty is a kindly, helpful bearing and a desire to scatter sunshine and good cheer everywhere, and this, shining through the face, makes it beautiful. The longing and the effort to be beautiful in character cannot fail to make the life beautiful, and since the outward is but an expression of the inward, a mere outpicturing on the body of the habitual thought and dominating motives, the face, the manners, and the bearing must follow the thought and become sweet and attractive. If you hold the beauty thought, the love thought, persistently in the mind, you will make such an impression of harmony and sweetness wherever you go that no one will notice any plainness or deformity of person.

There are girls who have dwelt upon what they consider their unfortunate plainness so long that they have seriously exaggerated it. They are not half so plain as they think they, are; and, were it not for the fact that they have made themselves very sensitive and self-conscious on the subject, others would not notice it at all. In fact, if they could get rid of their sensitiveness and be natural, they could, with persistent effort, make up in sprightliness of thought, in cheerfulness of manner, in intelligence, and in cheery helpfulness, what they lack in grace and beauty of face.

We admire the beautiful face, the beautiful form, but we love the face illumined by a beautiful soul. We love it because it suggests the ideal of the possible perfect man or woman, the ideal which was the Creator's model.

It is not the outward form of our dearest friend, but our ideal of friendship which he arouses or suggests in us that stirs up and brings into exercise our love and admiration. The highest beauty does not exist in the actual. It is the ideal, possible beauty, which the person or object symbolizes or suggests, that gives us delight.

Everyone should endeavor to be as beautiful, attractive, as complete a human being as possible. There is not a taint of vanity in the desire for the highest beauty.

The love of beauty that confines itself to mere external form, however, misses its deepest significance. Beauty of form, of coloring, of light and shade, of sound, make our world beautiful; yet the mind that is warped and twisted cannot see all this infinite beauty. It is the indwelling spirit, the ideal in the soul, that makes all things beautiful; that inspires and lifts us above ourselves.

We love the outwardly beautiful, because we crave perfection, and we cannot help admiring those persons and things that most nearly embody or measure up to our human ideal. But a beautiful character will make beauty and poetry out of the prosiest environment, bring sunshine into the darkest home, and develop beauty and grace amid the ugliest surroundings.

What would become of us if it were not for the great souls who realize the divinity of life, who insist upon bringing out and emphasizing its poetry, its music, its harmony and beauty?

How sordid and common our lives would become but for these beauty-makers, these inspirers, these people who bring out all that is best and most attractive in every place, every situation and condition.

There is no accomplishment, no trait of character, no quality of mind, which will give greater satisfaction and pleasure or contribute more to one's welfare than an appreciation of the beautiful. How many people might be saved from wrong-doing, even from lives of crime, by the cultivation of the esthetic faculties in their childhood! A love of the truly beautiful would save children from things which encoarsen and brutalize their natures. It would shield them from a multitude of temptations.

Parents do not take sufficient pains to develop a love and appreciation of beauty in their children. They do not realize that in impressionable youth, everything about the home, even the pictures, the paper on the wall, affect the growing character. They should never lose an opportunity

22

of letting their boys and girls see beautiful works of art, hear beautiful music; they should make a practise of reading to them or having them read very often some lofty poem, or inspirational passages from some great writer, that will fill their minds with thoughts of beauty, open their souls to the inflow of the Divine Mind, the Divine Love which encompasses us round about. 'The influences that move our youth determine the character, the success and happiness of our whole lives.

Every soul is born responsive to the beautiful, but this instinctive love of beauty must be fostered through the eye and the mind must be cultivated, or it will die. The craving for beauty is as strong in a child of the slums as in a favorite of fortune. "The physical hunger of the poor, the yearning of their stomachs," says Jacob A. Riis, "is not half so bitter, or so little likely to be satisfied as their esthetic hunger, their starving for the beautiful."

Mr. Riis has often tried to take flowers from his Long Island home to the "poors" in Mulberry Street, New York. "But they never got there," he says. "Before I had gone half a block from the ferry I was held up by a shrieky mob of children who cried for the posies and would not let me go another step till I had given them one. And when they got it they ran, shielding the flower with the most jealous care, to some place where they could hide and gloat over their treasure. They came dragging big, fat babies and little weazened ones that they might get a share, and the babies' eyes grew round and big at the sight of the golden glory from the fields, the like of which had never come their way. The smaller the baby, and the poorer, the more wistful its look, and so my flowers went. Who could have said them no?

"I learned then what I had but vaguely understood before, that there is a hunger that is worse than that which starves the body and gets into the newspapers. All children love beauty and beautiful things. It is the spark of the divine nature that is in them and justifies itself! To that ideal their souls grow. When they cry out for it they are trying to tell us in the only way they can that if we let the slum starve the ideal, with its dirt and its ugliness and its hard-trodden mud where flowers were meant to grow, we are starving that which we little know. A man, a human, may grow a big body without a soul; but as a citizen, as a mother, he or she is worth nothing to the commonwealth. The mark they are going to leave upon it is the black smudge of the slum.

"So when in these latter days we invade that slum to make homes there and teach the mothers to make them beautiful; when we gather the children into kindergartens, hang pictures in the schools; when we build beautiful new schools and public buildings and let in the light, with grass and flower and bird, where darkness and foulness were before; when we teach the children to dance and play and enjoy themselves alas! that it should ever be needed we are trying to wipe off the smudge, and to lift the heavy mortgage which it put on the morrow, a much heavier one in the loss of citizenship than any community, even the republic, can long endure. We are paying arrears of debt which we incurred by our sad neglect, and we could be about no better business."

There are many poor children in the slums of New York, Mr. Millionaire, who could go into your drawing-room and carry away from its rich canvases, its costly furnishings, a vision of beauty which you never perceived in them because your esthetic faculties, your finer sensibilities, were early stifled by your selfish pursuit of the dollar.

The world is full of beautiful things, but the majority have not been trained to discern them. We cannot see all the beauty that lies around us, because our eyes have not been trained to see it; our esthetic faculties have not been developed. We are like the lady who, standing with the great artist, Turrier, before one of his wonderful landscapes, cried out in amazement: "Why, Mr. Turner, I cannot see those things in nature that you have put in your picture."

"Don't you wish you could, madam?" he replied.

Just think what rare treats we shut out of our lives in our mad, selfish, insane pursuit of the dollar! Do you not wish that you could see the marvels that Turner saw in a landscape, that Ruskin saw in a sunset? Do you not wish that you had put a little more beauty into your life instead of allowing your nature to become encoarsened, your esthetic faculties blinded, and your finer instincts blighted by the pursuit of the coarser things of life; instead of developing your brute instincts of pushing and elbowing your way through the world for a few more dollars, in your selfish effort to get something away from somebody else?

Fortunate is the person who has been educated to the perception of beauty; he possesses a heritage of which no reverses can rob him. Yet it is a heritage possible to all who will take the trouble to begin early in life to cultivate the finer qualities of the soul, the eye, and the heart.

3
ENJOYING WHAT OTHERS OWN

If you are not wealthy yourself, be glad that somebody else
is, and you will be astonished at the happiness that will
result to yourself. REV. DR. CHARLES F. AKED.

"I would rather be able to appreciate things I cannot have
than to have things I am not able to appreciate."

IN his "Citizen of the World," Goldsmith describes a mandarin who appeared in a blaze of diamonds, and who was very ostentatiously thanked by a person in the crowd.

"What does the man mean?" the mandarin exclaimed. "Friend, I never gave thee any of my jewels." "No," replied the stranger, "but you have let me look at them; and that is all the use you can make of them yourself; so there is no difference between us, except that you have the trouble of watching them, and that is an employment I do not desire."

A French marquis with whom Washington Irving made us acquainted consoled himself for the loss of his chateau by remarking that he had Versailles and St. Cloud for his country resorts, and the shady alleys of the Tuileries and the Luxembourg for his town recreation.

"When I walk through these fine gardens," he said, "I have only to fancy myself the owner of them, and they are mine. All these gay crowds are my visitors, and I have not the trouble of entertaining them. My estate is a perfect Sans Souci, where everyone does as he pleases, and no one troubles the owner. All Paris is my theater, and presents me with a continual spectacle. I have a table spread for me in every street, and thousands of waiters ready to fly at my bidding. When my servants have waited upon me, I pay them, discharge them, and there's an end. I have no fears of their wronging or pilfering me when my back is turned. Upon the whole," said the old gentleman with a smile of infinite good humor, "when I recollect all that I have suffered, and consider all I at present enjoy, I can but look upon myself as a person of singular good fortune."

Robert L. Stevenson once packed up his pictures and his furniture and sent them to an enemy who was about to be married, and he wrote to a friend that he had at last rid him- self of his master, to whom he had been a bond slave. "Don't," he said, "give hostages to fortune, I implore you. Not once in a month will you be in a mood to enjoy a picture. When that mood comes, go to the gallery and see it. Meanwhile let some hired flunkey dust the picture and keep it in good condition for your coming."

How is it that some rare characters manage to have such precious treasures, so much that enriches the life, out of a poverty-stricken, forbidding environment, while others get little out of the most luxurious and beautiful conditions that wealth can furnish?

It is wholly a question of the quality of the absorbent material. Some people are blind to beauty. They can travel with the utmost indifference in the midst of the most gorgeous and inspiring scenery. Their souls are not touched. They do not feel the inspiration which puts others into ecstasy.

The power to absorb beauty depends on the quality of the mind to assimilate and incorporate it in the life.

I know a lady who has lived all her life in a poverty-stricken district, in the midst of squalor and all sorts of discord, and yet, in this miserable environment, she has developed a sweet and beautiful character. She possesses that marvelous soul-alchemy which transforms the common into the uncommon, the ugly into the beautiful, drudgery into delight.

Such rare characters are like the lily, which absorbs purity and beauty from the mud and slime of the swamp.

How few people extract from their environ ment and experience, even a tithe of their possibilities, either of happiness or of achievement!

Did you ever watch a bee flitting about gathering delicious honey from the most forbidding and unattractive sources? I know men and women who have this marvelous instinct for gathering honey from all sorts of sources, superbly developed. They extract it from the most repellent surroundings. They cannot talk with the poorest, meanest, most unfortunate specimen of humanity without getting that which will sweeten the life and enrich the experience.

The habit of feeling rich because you have developed the faculty of extracting wealth from everything you touch is riches indeed. Why should we not feel rich in all that our eyes can carry away, no matter if others happen to have the title-deed. Why should I not enjoy the beautiful gardens of the wealthy and their grounds, just as if I owned them? As I pass by I can make my own the wealth of color. The beauty of plants and lawn and flowers and trees are all mine. The title-deed of another does not cut off my esthetic ownership. The best part of the farm, the landscape, the beauty of the brook and the meadow, the slope of the valley, the song of the birds, the sunset cannot be shut up within the title-deed; they belong to the eye that can carry them away, the mind that can appreciate them.

Some people are so constituted that they do not need to Own things to enjoy them. There is no envy in their nature. They feel glad that others have money and a splendid home, even if they themselves live in poverty. Henry Ward Beecher had this broad, liberal, magnanimous, whole-hearted nature, which could enjoy without owning. He used to say that it was a great treat to him to go out and enjoy the good things in the shop windows, especially during the Christmas holidays, and he could make the architecture and sculpture of palatial homes his own and enjoy the grounds, no matter who had the title-deed to them.

This ability to gather enjoyment from all sorts of sources is a divine gift. It broadens the life, deepens the experience, and enriches the whole nature. It is a great force in self culture.

Some people are so mean and stingy, so uncharitable and narrow, so bigoted and suspicious, that they never open their natures wide enough to take in the riches all about them, the beauty with which they come in contact. They are so jealous and envious and small, that they are afraid to throw open the doors of their hearts. The result is, their lives are pinched and starved.

A person must be magnanimous and large hearted, to be able to absorb the wealth and beauty that are worthwhile.

I know a woman in New York who is a dwarf and a cripple, but who has such a sweet, open, beautiful nature that everybody loves her. She is welcome everywhere, because she loves everybody and feels interested in everyone. She is poor but she enters into other lives with a heartiness and unselfish abandonment and an enthusiasm that ought to shame those of us who are physically normal and in a better condition.

I knew a poor man who really enjoyed more than any rich man I know of, simply because early in life he learned to enjoy things without owning them to such an extent that he never seemed to have the slightest envy or jealousy in connection with them, but rather gratitude to those who owned them. He was such a sweet soul that all doors were open to him, because he radiated sunshine and good cheer.

It does not matter how poor or how unfortunate you are, you can enjoy, without the trouble of owning or caring for them, millions and millions of dollars' worth of works of art, and things of rarest beauty, almost as well as though they were your own. Think what it costs to maintain our great city parks, with all their wonders of beauty and comfort, the palatial public buildings, the fine residences, beautiful private grounds and gardens and objects of beauty everywhere, which you can enjoy without money, and yet you, perhaps, say you own nothing.

He has missed the finest lesson of culture and experience who has not learned how to enjoy without owning.

The secret of happiness is in a cheerful, contented mind. "He is poor who is dissatisfied; he is rich who is contented with what he has," and can enjoy what others own.

Children should be taught to feel rich in the wealth, goodness, beauty, and experiences of others, no matter how humble their own condition. It is a great thing to open up the nature while young, to keep all the avenues of one's heart wide open and responsive; to learn to be receptive, and to drink in everything that is good and true and beautiful which can enrich the nature and broaden the life.

4
PERSONALITY AS A SUCCESS ASSET

There is something about one's personality which eludes the photographer, which the painter cannot reproduce, which the sculptor cannot chisel. This subtle something which everyone feels, but which no one can describe, which no biographer ever put down in a book, has a great deal to do with one's success in life.

IT is this indescribable quality, which some persons have in a remarkable degree, which sets an audience wild at the mention of the name of a Blaine, a Lincoln, or a Roosevelt - which makes people applaud beyond the bounds of enthusiasm. It was this personal atmosphere which made Clay the idol of his constituents. Although, perhaps, Calhoun was a greater man, he never aroused any such enthusiasm as "the mill boy of the slashes." Webster and Sumner were great men, but they did not arouse a tithe of the spontaneous enthusiasm evoked by men like Blaine and Clay.

A historian says that, in measuring Kossuth's influence over the masses, "we must first reckon with the orator's physical bulk, and then carry the measuring line above his atmosphere." If we had discernment fine enough and tests delicate enough, we could not only measure the personal atmosphere of individuals, but could also make more accurate estimates concerning the future possibilities of schoolmates and young friends. We are often misled as to the position they are going to occupy from the fact that we are apt to take account merely of their ability, and do not reckon this personal atmosphere or magnetic power as a part of their. success-capital. Yet this individual atmosphere has quite as much to do with one's advancement as brain-power or education. Indeed, we constantly see men of mediocre ability but with 'fine personal presence, superb manner, and magnetic qualities, being rapidly advanced over the heads of those who are infinitely their superiors in mental endowments.

A good illustration of the influence of personal atmosphere is found in the orator who carries his audience with him like a whirlwind, while he is delivering his speech, and yet so little of his personal element adheres to his cold words in print that those who read them are scarcely moved at all. The influence of such speakers depends almost wholly upon their presence, the atmosphere that emanates from them.

Charm of personality is a divine gift that sways the strongest characters, and sometimes even controls the destinies of nations.

We are unconsciously influenced by people who possess this magnetic power. The moment we come into their presence we have a sense of enlargement. They unlock within us possibilities of which we previously had no conception. Our horizon broadens; we feel a new power stirring through all our being; we experience a sense of relief, as if a great weight which long had pressed upon us had been removed.

We can converse with such people in a way that astonishes us, although meeting them, perhaps, for the first time. We express ourselves more clearly and eloquently than we ever thought possible. They draw out the best that is in us; they introduce us, as it were, to our larger, better selves. In their presence, impulses and longings come thronging to our minds which never stirred us before. All at Once me takes on a higher and nobler meaning, and we are fired with a desire to do more than we have ever before done, and to be more than we have been in the past.

A few minutes before, perhaps, we were sad and discouraged, when, suddenly, the flashlight of a potent personality of this kind has opened a rift in our lives and revealed to us hidden capabilities. Sadness gives place to joy, despair to hope, and disheartenment to encouragement. We have been touched to finer issues; we have caught a glimpse of higher ideals; and, for the moment, at least, have been transformed. The old commonplace life, with its absence of purpose and endeavor, has dropped out of sight, and we resolve, with better heart and stronger hope, to struggle anew to make permanently ours the forces and potentialities that have been thus revealed to us.

Even a momentary contact with a character of this kind seems to double our mental and soul powers, as two great dynamos double the current which passes over the wire, and we are loath to leave the magical presence lest we lose our new-born power.

On the other hand, we frequently meet people who make us shrivel and shrink into ourselves. The moment they come near us we experience a cold chill, as if a blast of winter had struck us in midsummer. A blighting, narrowing sensation, which seems to make us suddenly smaller, passes over us. We feel a decided loss of power, of possibility. We could no more smile in their presence than we could laugh while at a funeral. Their gloomy, miasmatic atmosphere chills all our natural impulses. In their presence there is no possibility of expansion for us. As a dark cloud suddenly obscures the brightness of a smiling summer sky, their shadows are cast upon us and fill us with vague, indefinable uneasiness.

We instinctively feel that such people have no sympathy with our aspirations, and our natural prompting is to guard closely any expression of our hopes and ambitions. When they are near us our purposes and desires shrink, the charm of sentiment vanishes, and life seems to lose color and zest. The effect of their presence is paralyzing, and we hasten from it as soon as possible.

If we study these two types of personality, we shall find that the chief difference between them is that the first loves his kind, and the latter does not. Of course, that rare charm of manner which captivates all those who come within the sphere of its influence, and that strong personal magnetism which inclines all hearts toward its fortunate possessor, are largely natural gifts. But we shall find that the man who practises unselfishness, who is genuinely interested in the welfare of others, who feels it a privilege to have the power to do a fellow-creature a kindness, even though polished manners and a gracious presence may be absent, will be an elevating influence wherever he goes. He will bring encouragement and uplift to every life that touches his. He will be trusted and loved by all who come in contact with him. This type of superior personality we may all cultivate if we will.

This intangible, mysterious something, which we sometimes call individuality or personality, is often more powerful than the ability which can be measured, or the qualities that can be rated.

Many women are endowed with this magnetic quality, which is entirely independent of personal beauty. It is often possessed in a high degree by very plain women. This was notably the case with some of the women who ruled in the French *salons* more absolutely than the king on his throne.

At a social gathering, when conversation drags, and interest is at a low ebb, the entrance of some bright woman with a magnetic personality instantly changes the whole situation. She may not be handsome, but everybody is attracted to her; it is a privilege to converse with her.

People who possess this' rare quality are frequently ignorant of the source of their power. They simply know they have it, but cannot locate or describe it. While it is, like poetry, music, or art, a gift of nature, born in one, it can be cultivated.

Much of the charm of magnetic personality comes from a fine, cultivated manner. Tact, also, is a very important element, next to a fine manner, perhaps the most important. One must know exactly what to do, and be able to do just the right thing at the proper time. Good judgment and common sense are indispensable to those who are trying to acquire this magic power. Good taste is also one of the elements of personal charm. You cannot offend the tastes of others without hurting their sensibilities.

One of the greatest investments one can make is that of attaining a gracious manner, cordiality of bearing, generosity of feeling, the delightful art of pleasing. It is infinitely better than money capital, for all doors fly open to sunny, pleasing personalities. They are more than welcome; they are sought for everywhere.

Many a youth owes his promotion or his first start in life to the disposition to be accommodating, to help along wherever he could. This was one of Lincoln's chief characteristics; he had a passion for helping people, for making himself agreeable under all circumstances. Mr. Herndon, his law partner, says: "When the Rutledge Tavern, where Lincoln boarded, was crowded, he would often give up his bed, and sleep on the counter in his store with a roll of calico for his pillow. Somehow everybody in trouble turned to him for help." This generous desire to assist others and to return kindnesses endeared Lincoln to the people.

The power to please is a tremendous asset. What can be more valuable than a personality which always attracts, never repels? It is not only valuable in business, but also in every field of life. It makes statesmen and politicians; it brings clients to the lawyer, and patients to the physician. It is worth everything to the clergyman. No matter what career you enter, you cannot overestimate the importance of cultivating that charm of manner, those personal qualities, which attract people to you.

They will take the place of capital, or influence. They are often a substitute for a large amount of hard work.

Some men attract business, customers, clients, patients, as naturally as magnets attract particles of steel. Everything seems to point their way, for the same reason that the steel particles point toward the magnet, because they are attracted.

Such men are business magnets. Business moves toward them, even when they do not apparently make half so much effort to get it as the less successful. Their friends call them "lucky dogs." But if we analyze these men closely, we find that they have attractive qualities. There is usually some charm of personality about them that wins all hearts.

Many successful business and professional men would be surprised, if they should analyze their success, to find what a large percentage of it is due to their habitual courtesy and other popular qualities. Had it not been for these, their sagacity, long-headedness, and business training would not, perhaps, have amounted to half so much; for, no matter how able a man may be, if his coarse, rude manners drive away clients, patients, or customers, if his personality repels, he will always be placed at a disadvantage.

It pays to cultivate popularity. It doubles success possibilities, develops manhood, and builds up character. To be popular, one must strangle selfishness, he must keep back his bad tendencies, he must be polite, gentlemanly, agreeable, and companionable. In trying to be popular, he is on the road to success and happiness as well. The ability to cultivate friends is a powerful aid to success, It is capital which will stand by one when panics come, when banks fail, when business concerns go to the wall. How many men have been able to start again after having everything swept away by fire or flood, or some other disaster, just because they had cultivated popular qualities, because they had learned the art of being agreeable, of making friends and holding them with hooks of steel! People are influenced powerfully by their friendships, by their likes and dislikes, and a popular business or professional man has every advantage in the world over a cold, indifferent man, for customers, clients, or patients will flock to him.

Cultivate the art of being agreeable. It will help you to self-expression as nothing else will; it will call out your success qualities; it will broaden your sympathies. It is difficult to conceive of any more delightful birthright than to be born with this personal charm, and yet it is comparatively easy to cultivate, because it is made up of so many other qualities, all o-f which are cultivatable.

I never knew a thoroughly unselfish person who was not an attractive person. No person who is always thinking of himself and trying to figure out how he can get some advantage from everybody else will ever be attractive. We are naturally disgusted with people who are always trying to get everything for themselves and never think of anybody else.

The secret of pleasing is in being pleasant yourself, in being interesting. If you would be agreeable, you must be magnanimous. The narrow, stingy soul is not lovable. People shrink from such a character. There must be heartiness in the expression, in the smile, in the hand-shake, in the cordiality, which is unmistakable. The hardest natures cannot resist these qualities any more than the eyes can resist the sun. If you radiate sweetness and light, people will love to get near you, for we are all looking for the sunlight, trying to get away from the shadows.

It is unfortunate that these things are not taught more in the home and in the school; for our success and happiness depend largely upon them. Many of us are no better than uneducated heathens. We may know enough, but we give ourselves out stingily and we live narrow and reserved lives, when we should be broad, generous, sympathetic, and magnanimous.

Popular people, those with great personal charm, take infinite pains to cultivate all the little graces and qualities which go to make up popularity. If people who are naturally unsocial would only spend as much time and take as much pains as people who are social favorites in making themselves popular, they would accomplish wonders.

Everybody is attracted by lovable qualities and is repelled by the unlovely, wherever found. The whole principle of an attractive personality lies in this sentence: A fine manner pleases; a coarse, brutal manner repels. We cannot help being attracted to one who is always trying to help us, who gives us his sympathy, who is always trying to make us comfortable and to give us every advantage he can. On the other hand, we are repelled by people who are always trying to get something out of us, who elbow their way in front of us to get the best seat in a car or a hall, who are always looking for the easiest chair, or for the choicest bits at the table, who are always wanting to be waited on first at the restaurant or hotel, regardless of others.

The ability to bring the best that is in you to the man you are trying to reach, to make a good impression at the very first meeting, to approach a prospective customer as though you had known him for years without offending his taste, without raising the least prejudice, but getting his sympathy and good will, is a great accomplishment, and' this is what commands a great salary.

It is one of the most difficult things in the world to change our first impression of a person, whether good or bad. We do not realize how rapidly the mind works when we meet anyone for the first time. We are all eyes and ears; our mind is busy weighing the person upon the scales of our judgment. We are all alert, watching for earmarks of strength or weakness. Every word, every act, the manner, the voice, the mind takes in everything very rapidly, and our judgment is not only formed quickly, but also firmly, so that it is very difficult and almost impossible for us to get this first picture of the person entirely out of our mind.

Careless, tactless people are often obliged to spend a great deal of time in trying to overcome the bad first impressions they make. They apologize and explain in letters. But apology and explanation usually have very little effect, because they are so much weaker than the strong picture of the first impression which frequently persists in spite of all efforts to change it. Hence it is of the utmost importance for a youth who is trying to establish himself to be very careful of the impression he makes. A bad first impression may be the means of barring him from credit.

There is a charm in a gracious personality from which it is very hard to get away. It is difficult to snub the man who possesses it. There is something about him which arrests your prejudice, and no matter how busy or how worried you may be, or how much you may dislike to be interrupted, somehow you haven't the heart to turn away the man with a pleasing personality.

. Who has not felt his power multiplied many times, his intellect sharpened, and a keener edge put on all of his faculties, when coming in contact with a strong personality which knowledge is valuable, but the knowledge which comes from mind intercourse is invaluable.

Two substances totally unlike, but having a chemical affinity for each other, may produce a third infinitely stronger than either, or even both, of those which unite. Two people with a strong affinity often call into activity in each other a power which neither dreamed he possessed before. Many an author owes his greatest book, his cleverest saying to a friend who has aroused in him latent powers which otherwise might have remained dormant. Artists have been touched by the power of inspiration through a masterpiece, or by someone they happened to meet who saw in them what no one else had ever seen,-the power to do an Immortal thing.

The man who mixes with his fellows is ever on a voyage of discovery, finding new islands of power in himself which would have remained forever hidden but for association with others. Everybody he meets has some secret for him, if he can only extract it, something which he never knew before, something which will help him on his way, something which will enrich his life. No man finds himself alone. Others are his discoverers.

It is astonishing how much you can learn from people in social intercourse when you know how to look at them rightly. But it is a fact that you can only get a great deal out of them by giving them a great deal of yourself. The more you radiate yourself, the more magnanimous you are, the more generous *of* yourself, the more you fling yourself out to them without reserve, the more you will get back.

You must give much in order to get much. The current will not set toward you until it goes out from you. About all you get from others is a reflex of the currents from yourself. The more generously you give, the more you get in return. You will not receive generously if you give out stingily, narrowly, meanly. You must give of yourself in a wholehearted, generous way, or you will receive only stingy rivulets, when you might have had great rivers and torrents of blessings.

A man who might have been symmetrical, well-rounded, had he availed himself of every opportunity to touch life along all sides, remains a pygmy in everything except his own little specialty, because he did not cultivate his social side.

It is always a mistake to miss an opportunity to meet with our kind, and especially to mix with those who are above us, because we can always carry away something of value. It is through social intercourse that our rough corners are rubbed off, that we become polished and attractive.

If you go into social life with a determination to give it something, to make it a school for self-improvement, for calling out your best social qualities, for developing the latent brain cells, which have remained dormant from the lack of exercise, you will not find society either a bore or unprofitable. But you must give it something, or you will not get anything.

When you learn to look upon everyone you meet as holding a treasure, something which will enrich your life, which will enlarge and broaden your experience, and make you more of a man, you will not think the time in the drawing-room wasted.

The man who is determined to get on will look upon every experience as an educator, as a culture chisel, which will make his life a little more shapely and attractive.

Frankness of manner is one of the most delightful of traits in young or old. Every body admires the open-hearted, the people who have nothing to conceal, and who do not try to cover up their faults and weaknesses. They are, as a rule, large-hearted and magnanimous. They inspire love and confidence, and, by their very frankness and simplicity, invite the same qualities in others.

Secretiveness repels as much as frankness attracts. There is something about the very inclination to conceal or cover up which arouses suspicion and distrust. We cannot have the same confidence in people who possess this trait, no matter how good they may seem to be, as in frank, sunny natures. Dealing with these secretive people is like traveling on a stage coach on a dark night. There is always a feeling of uncertainty. We may come out all right, but there is a lurking fear of some pitfall or unknown danger ahead of us. 'We are uncomfortable because of the uncertainties. They may be all right, and may deal squarely with us, but we are not sure and cannot trust them. No matter how polite or gracious a secretive person may be, we can never rid ourselves of the feeling that there is a motive behind his graciousness, and that he has an ulterior purpose in view. He is always more or less of an enigma, because he goes through life wearing a mask. He endeavors to hide every trait that is not favorable to himself. Never, if he can help it, do we get a glimpse of the real man.

How different the man who comes out in the open, who has no secrets, who reveals his heart to us, and who is frank, broad, and liberal! How quickly he wins 'our confidence! How we all like and trust him. We forgive him for many a slip or weakness, because he is always ready to confess his faults, and to make amends for them. If he has bad qualities, they are always in sight, and we are ready to make allowances for them. His heart is sound and true, his sympathies are broad and active. The very qualities he possesses frankness and simplicity are conducive to the growth of the highest manhood.

In the Black Hills of South Dakota there lived a humble, ignorant miner, who won the love and good will of everyone. "You can't 'elp likin' 'im," said an English miner; and when asked why the miners and the people in the town couldn't help liking him, he answered: "Because he has a 'eart in 'im; he's a man. He always helps the boys when in trouble. You never go to 'im for nothin'."

Bright, handsome young men, graduates of Eastern colleges, were there seeking their fortune; a great many able, strong men drawn there from different parts of the· country by the gold fever; but none of them held the public confidence like this poor man. He could scarcely write his name, and knew nothing of the usages of polite society, yet he so intrenched himself in the hearts in his community that no other man, however educated or cultured, had the slightest chance of being elected to any office of prominence while "Ike" was around.

He was elected mayor of his town, and sent. to the legislature, although he could not speak a grammatical sentence. It was all because he had" a 'eart in 'im"; he was a man.

5
HOW TO BE A SOCIAL SUCCESS

The power to please is a great success asset. It will do for you what money will not do. It will often give you capital which your financial assets alone would not warrant. People are governed by their likes and dislikes. We are powerfully influenced by a pleasing, charming personality. A persuasive manner is often irresistible. Even judges on the bench feel its fascination.

LORD CHESTERFIELD has called the art of pleasing one of the choicest gifts. It is a great social power. If you want to be popular, you must assume a popular attitude, and, above all, you must be interesting. If people are not interested in you, they will avoid you. But if you can be so sunny and cheerful, helpful and kind, if you can fling sunshine about you in every direction, so that people will cross the street to meet you, instead of trying to avoid you, you will have no difficulty in becoming popular.

The best way to draw people to you is to make them feel that you are interested in them. You must not do this for effect. You must be really interested in them, or they will detect the deception.

Nothing else will win the heart of a young person to you so quickly as making him feel that you take a genuine interest in him, in what he is doing, and especially in what he is going to do in the future.

If you avoid people, you must expect them to avoid you; and if you always talk about yourself and your wonderful achievements, you will find that people will move away from you. You do not please them. They want you to talk about them, to be interested in that which concerns them.

If you wear a bulldog expression, if you go about looking sour and disagreeable, you must not wonder that you are not popular with your employees or other people. Everybody likes a pleasant face. We are always looking for the sunshine, and we want to get away from the clouds and gloom.

There are many people who think that much of what is real culture and refinement is merely affectation. They believe that a diamond in the rough is the only genuine diamond. If a man is sincere, they argue, if he possesses manly qualities and is loyal to truth, no matter how uncouth and coarse he may be outwardly, he will be respected and will be successful.

This argument is good only to a limited extent. What is true of an uncut gem is also true of a human diamond in the rough. No matter how intrinsically valuable they may be, no one would think of wearing uncut diamonds. A man might have a million dollars' worth of such gems; yet, if he refused to have them cut and polished, no one would appreciate them. The unpractised eye would not be able to distinguish' them from common pebbles. They are valuable only in proportion to the degree of brilliancy and beauty which the diamond-cutter can call out of them.

So, a man may be possessed of many admirable qualities, but, if they are covered by a rough, uncouth exterior, they will be robbed of much of their intrinsic value. They will be discovered only by keen observers, or expert character readers. What cutting and polishing do for crystalized carbon, education and refined social intercourse do for the human diamond in the rough. The grace of fine culture, a charming personality, and an exquisite manner enhance its value a thousandfold.

****

I know a man a type of thousands of others, who cannot understand why people avoid him. If he is at a social gathering everybody seems repelled from his side of the room. When others are enjoying themselves, chatting and laughing, he is silent, in a corner by himself. If, by any accident, he gets into the center of attraction, there seems to be a centrifugal force acting upon him, which quickly draws him out again to his solitary corner. He is rarely invited anywhere. He appears to be a social icicle, there is no warmth about him, no magnetism.

The reason for this man's unpopularity is a mystery to him. He has great ability, is a hard worker, and, when his day's work is done, likes to relax and mingle with his kind; but he gets none of the pleasure for which he longs. He is mortified to find himself persistently shunned while others, with not a tithe of his ability, are welcomed wherever they go. He has no idea that selfishness is the principal bar to his popularity. He is always thinking of self. He cannot get himself or his business out of his mind long enough to take an interest in other people or their affairs. No matter how often you talk with him, he always wants to pull the conversation around to himself or his business.

Another hindrance to his social success is that he does not know the secret of attraction. He does not know that every person is a magnet, which attracts in exact intensity and power to the habitual thought and motive. The man who is always thinking of himself becomes a self-magnet, attracting himself, nobody else. Many men become money magnets. Their thoughts have been held on money so long that they attract money, nothing else. Some men become vicious because they have made themselves vice magnets.

On the other hand, there are men and women so beautiful in mind and in character that everybody who comes in contact with them feels a sense of ownership or close kinship with them. Everyone about them loves and admires them. These large-hearted creatures are loved because they love. They are magnets which attract all sorts of people because they are large enough to take them in. They are interested in them all; they have charity for everyone.

We instinctively measure the predominating qualities of a person, and estimate everything about him, under favorable conditions. We perceive his dominating qualities and know at once whether he is a Chinese wall of exclusiveness, or don't-touch-me-ness, or a generous, open, magnanimous nature, without bars, or secrets, or evasiveness, one who attracts and loves everybody else.

As long as a man remains cold, self-centered, and self-contemplative, he will have no magnetism for others. He will be shunned and disliked. No one will voluntarily seek him. It is just a question of the kind of magnet he makes of himself. The moment he shows regard for and interest in others, he will take on magnetic qualities, and attract, where before he repelled. He will draw others to him just in proportion to his interest in them. As soon as he puts himself in another's place, takes a genuine interest in his welfare, and does not try to shift the conversation to himself and his own affairs, just so soon and no sooner will others take an interest in him. There is only way to win love, and that is to love. Love will break the bonds of selfishness and self-consciousness. Stop thinking of self, and take an interest in others; develop an admiration and love for them, a real desire to help them, and you will not fail to be loved and to be popular.

Many persons are avoided because they are always shut up within themselves, absorbed in their own affairs. They have lived with themselves so long that they have lost connection and sympathy with the outside world. They have lived a subjective life so long that an objective one seems impossible. They did not realize that living alone and not interesting themselves in others for years would shut off their powers of attraction and dry up their sympathies, until they would cease to generate any warmth or power, and would become human icicles, so cold that their mere presence would chill the whole atmosphere about them.

Man is so constituted that he does not live normally alone. A large part of the best of his life comes from others. He is a related being, and, when cut off from his fellows, loses half his power. As a rule, a man is great only as he comes so in contact with other lives that there is a vital pulsating connection between himself and other men, and their lives and thoughts surge through him, and his through them.

The moment a cluster of green grapes is severed from the parent stem it begins to shrivel. The moment the sap which feeds it is cut off, it grows stale and insipid. It becomes worthless. The virtue of the cluster comes from its sap connection, its nourishment connection with the soil through the main vine. It can do nothing alone. When its source of power is cut off, it ceases to grow. It dies.

A man is but a cluster on the great human grapevine. He begins to dry up the moment he is cut off from his fellows. There is something in the Solidarity of the human race which cannot be accounted for in the sum total of all the individuals. As Kipling says: "The strength of the wolf is in the pack." Separation from the mass involves a mighty loss of power in the individual, just as there is a loss of cohesion and adhesion involved in the separation of the molecules and atoms of the diamond. The value of the gem is in the close contact, the compactness, and the concentration of the particles which compose it. The moment they are separated its value is gone. So a strong, effective man gets a large part of his strength from the vital connection with his fellows.

Man is omnivorous mentally as well as physically. He requires a variety of mental food, which he can obtain only by mixing with a great variety of people. The moment a human being is separated from his kind, he begins to deteriorate. Children who have been imprisoned and kept many years from all communication with other human beings have deteriorated to idiocy.

A man is strong in proportion to the quantity, the quality, and the variety of forces which he absorbs from others. He is a power in proportion to the extent of his contact, socially, mentally, and morally, with his kind, and a weakling just in proportion as he cuts himself off from others.

Some religious organizations have tried to evolve moral giants by separating the individuals in monasteries or cloisters, by cutting off all communication with the outside world and practically also with one another.

But their method has proven a failure, as have all plans which have interfered with the Creator's great plan of human solidarity.

There is a mighty telepathic force, playing between brain and brain, between soul and soul, which we do not yet know how to measure, but it is powerful to stimulate, mighty to build up or to tear down. There are scores of avenues which carry nutriment to the human mind, and to close up any of them must result in dwarfing the faculties, in shutting off power. The five senses are only a small number of the vehicles which carry impressions and information to the inner man. There are other, intangible, unknown soul senses, which illuminate the mind. We grow largely upon the nutriment which the soul absorbs from everywhere, but which the crude senses cannot weigh or measure. We drink in power through the eye and ear which does not Come through the optic or auditory nerves. The greatest thing which comes from a master painting is not in the tints or the shades or forms on the canvas, but is back of all that, in the artist, a mighty force which inheres in his personality, is made up of the sum of all he has inherited and all he has experienced. Who can ever measure the suggestive force which reaches the inner consciousness through the imagination?

An opportunity to associate with people who see the best instead of the worst in us is worth far, far more to us than an opportunity to make money. It increases a hundredfold our power to develop noble characters.

Beware of people who are constantly belittling others, finding flaws and defects in their characters, or slyly insinuating that they are not quite what they ought to be. Such persons are dangerous, and not to be trusted. A disparaging mind is a limited, rutty; unhealthy mind. It can neither see nor acknowledge good in others. It is a jealous mind: it is really painful to it to hear others spoken well of, praised, or commended for any virtue or good point. If it cannot deny the existence of the alleged good, it will seek to minimize it by a malicious "if," or "but," or try in some other way to throw a doubt on the character of the person praised.

A large, healthy, normal mind will see the good in another much more quickly than the evil, but a narrow, belittling mind has an eye only for faults, for the unlovely and the crooked. The clean, the beautiful, the true, and the magnanimous are too large for its vision. It delights in tearing down or destroying, but it is incapable of upbuilding.

Whenever you hear a person trying to belittle another, discard him from your list of friends, unless you can help him to remedy his fault. Do not flatter yourself that those who tell you of the failings of other people, and criticize and hold them up to ridicule, will not treat you in the same way when an opportunity presents itself. Such people are incapable of true friendship, for true friendship helps, instead of hinders; it never exposes the weak point in a friend's character, or suffers anyone to speak ill of him.

One of the finest fruits of culture is the power to see the man or woman whom God made in his own image, and not the one who is scarred by faults and deficiencies. It is only the generous, loving soul who ever attains to this degree of culture. It is only the broad, charitable, magnanimous, great-hearted man or woman who is blind to the defects of others, and always ready to enlarge upon their good qualities.

We are all of us constantly, but unconsciously, molding others by our thoughts about them. The qualities you see in your friend and those with whom you come in contact, you tend to enlarge. If you see only the little, mean, contemptible side of people.. you cannot help them out of their faults, for you only intensify and fix them; but if you see the good, the noble, the aspiring traits in them, you will help to develop these qualities until they crowd out the base, unworthy ones.

Everywhere, the world over, this unconscious interchange of influence is at work, hindering or helping according to its nature.

Many people become morbid in dwelling upon the thought that they are peculiar in some respect. Some of these people think they have inherited certain tendencies or peculiarities from their parents and are always looking for their reappearance in themselves. Now this is just the way to make them appear, for what we encourage in the mind or hold there persistently we draw to us. So these people continually increase the evil by worrying about it and dwelling upon its sad effects on themselves. They become sensitive about real or imaginary idiosyncrasies. They never like to speak of or hear of them, and yet the belief that they possess them takes away their self-confidence and mars their achievement.

Most of these peculiarities are usually imaginary or are exaggerated by imagination. But they have been nursed and brooded over so long that they have become real to the sufferers.

The remedy lies in doing precisely the opposite, dwelling on the perfect qualities and ignoring any possible shortcomings. If you think you are peculiar, form a habit of holding the normal thought. Say to yourself, "I am not peculiar. The idiosyncrasies that ·disturb me are not real. I was made in the image of my Maker, and a Perfect Being could not make imperfections, hence the imperfections I think I have cannot be real, as the truth of my being is real. There can be no abnormalities about me unless I produce them in thought, for the Creator never gave them to me. He never gave me a discordant note, because He is Harmony."

If you hold this thought persistently in mind, you will forget what seems abnormal to you; it will soon disappear and you will regain your confidence just by becoming convinced that you are not much unlike other people.

Shyness sometimes becomes a disease; but it is a disease of the imagination only, and can be easily overcome by driving the thought of it out of the mind and holding the opposite thought, by one's just making up his mind that he is not being watched by everybody and that people are too busy about their own selfish aims and ambitions to be observing him all the time.

I know a girl who had become so morbid and despondent, through constantly dwelling on her plain features and ungainly manner, that she was on the verge of insanity. She was extremely sensitive, very proud, and would brood for days over the fancied slight when she was not invited to a party or other entertainment with her more attractive acquaintances.

Finally a real friend came to her assistance, and told her that it was possible for her to cultivate qualities which would be far more attractive and would make her much more popular than the mere physical beauty and grace whose absence she so deplored.

With this kind friend's assistance she completely reversed her estimate of herself; she turned about face, and, instead of over-emphasizing mere physical grace and beauty, instead of thinking of herself as ugly and repulsive, she constantly held the thought that she was the expression of God's idea, that there was something divine in her, and she resolved to bring it out.

She denied every suggestion that she could possibly be unpopular, or that she could really be ugly, and held persistently in mind the image of her popularity and attractiveness, and the thought that she could make herself interesting and even fascinating. She would not allow herself to harbor the suggestion that she could be anything but attractive.

She began to improve herself intellectually in every possible way. She read the best authors; she took up different courses of study; and determined that at every opportunity she would make herself just as interesting as possible.

Hitherto she had been careless in her dress and manners because of the conviction that it did not matter how she dressed or what she did, for she would still be unpopular. She began to dress as becomingly as possible and in better taste.

The result was, that, instead of being a wallflower, as formerly, she began to attract little groups about her wherever she went. She became a fascinating talker, and made herself so interesting in every way that she was invited out just as often as the more attractive girls whom she used to envy. In a short time she had not only overcome her handicap, but had also become the most interesting girl in her community.

Her task had not been an easy one, but she had worked with superb resolution and grit to overcome the things which had held her down; and,

47

in her determined effort to overcome what she regarded as a fatal handicap, as a curse, she was enabled to develop qualities which more than compensated for the personal beauty that was denied her.

It is wonderful what a transformation we can bring about by holding persistently in the mind the image of the thing we desire or would become, and struggling hard to attain it. This has a marvelous power to attract what we desire, to make real the picture that we see.

The speaking voice has much to do with one's popularity and social success. There is no one thing which marks the degree of good breeding, culture, and refinement so much as a sweet, modulated, cultivated voice.

"Shut me up in a dark room with a mixed multitude," says Thomas Wentworth Higginson, "and I can pick out the gentlefolks by their voices."

It is said that during the early history of Egypt only written pleadings were allowed in the law courts, lest the judges on the bench might be influenced or swayed by the eloquence of the human voice. In announcing the verdict, the presiding judge, with an image of the goddess of Truth, merely touched in silence the person on trial.

Considering the marvelous power of the human voice is it not a shame, almost a crime, that our children at home and in the public schools should not have their voices well trained? Is it not pitiable to see a bright, promising child getting a good education and yet developing a harsh, coarse, strident, nasal, disagreeable voice, which will handicap his whole career? Think of what a handicap this is to a girl!

But in America one finds boys and girls graduated from schools and colleges, institutions supposed to have taught them how to make the most and best of life, instructed in the dead languages, in mathematics, in the sciences, art, and literature, yet with voices 'rasping, nasal, repellent.

Many brilliant young women, who have been graduated with degrees from universities, possess voices so discordant and harsh that a person with sensitive nerves can scarcely carryon a conversation with them.

What is so fascinating, so charming, as the human voice when properly modulated and when properly trained? It is a real treat to listen to a voice that enunciates clearly, flings out the words clean-cut, liquid, and musical, as from a divine instrument.

I know a lady whose voice has such a charm that wherever she goes everyone listens whenever she speaks, because they cannot help it. Her voice simply captivates one. Her features are plain, almost to the point of ugliness, but her voice is divine; the charm is irresistible, and indicative of her highly cultivated mind and charming character.

I have heard female voices in society which were so high-keyed, which rasped so terribly upon the nerves, and so offended the sensibilities, that I have been obliged, time and again, to retreat from their reach.

A pure, low-keyed, trained voice, which breathes of culture and refinement, and gives out clean-cut words and sentences and syllables with perfect enunciation, a voice which expresses the very soul, rising and falling in sweet undulations that captivate, is a divine possession possible to most persons, especially women.

6
THE MIRACLE OF TACT

"Talent is something, but tact is everything." "Talent is no match for tact; we see its failure everywhere. In the race of life, common sense has the right of way."

TACT is an extremely delicate quality, difficult to define, hard to cultivate, but absolutely indispensable to one who wishes to get on in the world rapidly and smoothly.

Some people possess this exquisite sense in such a degree that they never offend, and yet they say everything that they wish to. They apparently do not restrain themselves, and say things with impunity which, if said by many others, would give mortal offense.

On the other hand, certain people, no matter what they say, cannot seem to avoid irritating the sensitiveness of others, although they mean well. Such people go through life misunderstood, for they cannot quite adjust themselves to circumstances. The way is never quite clear. They are continually running against something. They are always causing offense without meaning to, uncovering blemishes or sore spots. They invariably appear at the wrong time and do the wrong thing. They never get hold of the right end of the thread, so that the skein does not unravel, but the more they pull, the worse they tangle the threads.

Who can estimate the loss to the world which results from the lack of tact, the blundering, the stumbling, the slips, the falls, the fatal mistakes which come to people because they do not know how to do the right thing at the right time! How often we see splendid ability wasted, or not used effectively, because people lack this indefinable, exquisite quality which we call "tact."

You may have a college education; you may have a rare training in your specialty; you may be a genius in certain lines, and yet not get on in the world; but if you have tact and one talent combined with stick-to-it-iveness, you will be promoted, you will surely climb.

No matter how much ability a man may have, if he lacks the tact to direct it effectively, to say the right thing and to do the right thing at just the right time, he cannot make it effective.

Thousands of people accomplish more with small ability and great tact than those with great ability and little tact.

Everywhere we see people tripping themselves up, making breaks which cost friendships, customers, money, simply because they have never developed this faculty. Merchants are losing customers; lawyers, influential clients; physicians, patients; editors sacrificing subscribers; clergyman losing their power in the pulpit and their hold upon the public; teachers losing their situations; politicians losing their hold upon the people, because of the lack of tact.

Tact is a great asset in business, especially for a merchant. In a large city where hundreds of concerns are trying to attract the customer's attention, tact plays a very important part.

One prominent business man puts tact at the head of the list in his success recipe, the other three things being: enthusiasm, knowledge of business, dress.

The following paragraph, in a letter which a merchant sent out to his customers, is an example of shrewd business tact:

"We should be thankful for any information of any dissatisfaction with any former transactions with us, and we will take immediate steps to remedy it."

Think of the wealthy customers that have been driven away from banks by the lack of tact on the part of a cashier or teller!

A man must possess the happy faculty of winning the confidence of his fellow-beings and making steadfast friends, if he would be successful in his business or profession. Good friends praise our books at every opportunity, "talk up" our wares, expatiate at length on our last case in court, or on our efficiency in treating some patient; they protect our name when slandered, and rebuke our maligners. Without tact, the gaining of friends who will render such services is impossible.

A young man with very ordinary ability gained a seat in the United States Senate largely because of his wonderful tact.

A great many men are held down, kept back, because they cannot get along well with others. They are so constituted that they nettle

51

others, run against their prejudices. They cannot seem to cooperate with other people. The result is they have to work alone, and they lose the strength which comes from solidarity.

I know a man whose effectiveness during a very strenuous life has been almost ruined by the lack of tact. He can never get along with people. He seems to have every other quality necessary to make a large man, a leader of men, but his faculty for antagonizing others has crippled his life. He is always doing the wrong thing, saying the wrong thing, hurting people's feelings without meaning to, counteracting the 'effectiveness of his own work, because he has not the slightest appreciation of what the word tact means. He is constantly giving offense.

We all know men who pride themselves on saying what they think, on being blunt. They think it is honest, a sign of strength of character; and that it is weak to "beat about the bush" and to resort to diplomacy in dealing with people. They believe in "striking right out from the shoulder," "calling things by their right names."

These men have never been much of a success. People believe them to be honest, but their lack of tact, good judgment, and good sense is all the time queering their propositions. They do not know how to manage people, cannot get along with them, and are always" in hot water."

The truth is, we all like to be treated with consideration, with tact, and to deal with people who use diplomacy. Diplomacy IS common-sense reduced to a fine art.

Bluntness is a quality which people do not like or appreciate. People who pride themselves on saying just what they think, do not usually have a great many friends, nor a very large business or successful profession. Often truths which will hurt are better unsaid.

Mark Twain says: "Truth is so very precious that we should use it sparingly."

"A man may have not much learning nor wit," says Addison, "but if he has commonsense and something friendly in his behavior, it will conciliate men's minds more than the brightest thoughts without this disposition."

"A little management may often have resistance which a vast force may vainly strive to overcome," says another writer.

To quote again:

"A tactful man will not only make the most of everything he does know, but also of many things he does not know, and will gain more credit by his adroit mode of hiding his ignorance than a pedant by his attempt to exhibit his erudition."

When the French Revolution was at its height and the exciting mob was surging through the Paris streets, a detachment of soldiers filled one of the streets and a commanding officer was about to order his men to fire, when a young lieutenant asked permission to appeal to the people. Riding out in front of the soldiers, he doffed his hat and said: "Gentlemen will have the kindness to retire, for I am ordered to shoot down the rabble." The mob at once dispersed as if by magic, and the street was cleared without bloodshed.

Tact enabled Lincoln to extricate himself from a thousand unfortunate and painful situations with politicians during the Civil War. In fact, without it, the result of the war might have been entirely changed.

"The kindly element of humor almost always enters into the use of tact, and sweetens its mild coercion. We cannot help smiling, oftentimes, at the deft way in which we have been induced to do what we afterwards recognize as altogether right and best. There need be no deception in this use of tact, only such a presentation of rightful inducements as shall most effectively appeal to a hesitating mind. It is the fine art of getting the right thing done in the nick of time."

Someone has said, "Every fish has its fly."

As every fish has its fly, so every person can be reached, no matter how odd or peculiar, by the person who has tact enough to touch him in the right place.

A teacher in one of the public schools re proved a little eight-year-old Irish boy for some mischief. The boy was about to deny the fault when the teacher said, "I saw you, Jerry." "Yes," replied the boy as quick as a flash, " I tells them there ain't much you don't see with them purty black eyes of yours."

Tactful people make friends rapidly because they have a way of drawing people out and inducing them to express the best within them.

We always admire people who interest themselves in our affairs and who are not forever trying to talk about themselves and their own interests.

When William Penn went to pay his respects to Charles II, true to his Quaker principles, he kept on his hat. But the Merry Monarch, instead of showing anger, respectfully doffed his. "Prithee, Friend Charles, put on thy hat," said the great Friend; "N o, Friend Penn," replied the king, "it is usual for only one man to stand covered here."

King Edward, when a prince, was the most popular man in the United Kingdom, because of his never-failing tact and urbanity.

Some people seem to be incapable of learning tactfulness, because they do not appreciate delicate situations. They are often thick skinned themselves and cannot understand sensitive people.

A lady who had been a guest in a country home wrote to her hostess saying what a nice visit she had had, and that she was all right except that her hand was sore from mosquito bites, and that it did seem good to get back once more to a comfortable bathroom.

Someone has said, "The secret of all success lies in being alive to what is going on around one; in adjusting oneself to one's surroundings; in being sympathetic and helpful; in knowing the wants of the time; in saying to one's fellows what they want to hear, what they need to hear at the right moment .

It is not enough to do the right thing; it must be done at the right time and place."

Tact is a combination of good temper, ready wit, quickness of perception, and ability to take in the exigency of the occasion instantly. It is never offensive, but is a balm allaying suspicion, and soothing. It is appreciative. It is plausible without being dishonest, apparently consults the welfare of the second party and does not manifest any selfishness. It is never antagonistic, never opposes, never strokes the hair the wrong way, and never irritates.

Tact, like a fine manner eases the way, takes the jar out of the jolts; oils the bearings, opens doors barred to others; sits in the drawing-room when others must wait in the reception hall; gets into the private office when others are turned down. It admits you into exclusive circles, where wealth abounds, even though poor. It secures the position when merit is turned away.

Tact is a great manager; it easily controls people, even when combined with small ability, where genius cannot get along.

With tact, one woman, even with mediocre ability, is able to be a leader in society and wield great influence over statesmen and brilliant men in all vocations, while another woman very much her superior in other intellectual endowments remains in obscurity and apparently without influence, because she lacks this exquisite quality.

I was once in a home where the wife used to perform what to me seemed almost a daily miracle. The husband would come to breakfast always in a great rush, with his paper in his hand, cross and crabbed from his perplexing business and late hours at the club.

He was a very nervous man, and everything seemed to irritate him in the morning. He was always late at breakfast, and if everything was not ready on the instant, piping hot, he would fly into a rage, which, but for the wife's marvelous tact, would have destroyed the peace and comfort of the family for the entire day. The servants stood in fear of their master, because they dreaded his tongue lashings, his hot temper.

The calm, serene, gentle wife, however, was usually equal to the emergency. No matter where the trouble was, with marvelous tact and gentleness she would slip in and calm the storm. If the husband's coffee did not please him, she would immediately remove his cup, go to the kitchen, and in a few minutes return with a fresh, deliciously creamed, boiling hot cup, which would temporarily quiet her bear husband.

This man would sometimes throw food that did not suit him across the dining-room in his fits of anger. But the patient wife would make excuses that her husband's business was very trying, and that he had not been well of late.

Sometimes he was so domineering that the servants threatened to leave immediately; but the wife in her tactful manner would smooth everything over.

She always seemed to be equal to any emergency, and usually managed to calm the storm, to pour the oil of gentleness and sweetness upon the troubled waters. She went about the home like a ray of sunshine, shedding light, warmth, and beauty everywhere.

Many a patient has lost his life for the lack of tact in physician or relatives. A patient ought to be benefited by a visit from a physician even without medicine. A physician ought to be so cheerful, buoyant, exuberant with life, that his very presence would cheer the patient, give hope and encouragement. A gloomy, sad-faced, moody, tactless physician is a poor health restorer. Only those who are happy and cheerful should administer to the unfortunate sick. The personality of a physician has a great deal to do with his success, and with the chances of his patients.

Everything which tends to depress and discourage and take away hope should be kept away from the ill. The coming of the physician ought to be a signal of encouragement. Hope and confidence should come with him. He should radiate cheerfulness, encouragement. A brutal, coarse physician is a calamity to any community. In fact, a physician's personality and his tact are often much more important than his remedies.

Some physicians are so conscientious and so tactless, that they think they must tell patients the whole truth when they believe they cannot recover, instead of giving them the benefit of the doubt, for every physician knows that, nearly always, there is a doubt which way the case will turn. Cheerful encouragement has saved many a life by helping it to pass a crisis favorably, when the actual truth might have killed the patient or reduced his rallying powers to the danger-point. In all the affairs of life, cruel bluntness in stating brutal facts has caused untold misery and broken many friendships.

Napoleon actually terrified ladies by his coarse brutality and his selfishness in conversation.

He once said to one of the most beautiful, courtly women of his time, Madame Reynault, in a large company and in hearing of court ladies who were envious of her, "Do you know, Madame, you are aging terribly?" She was only twenty-eight and replied with exquisite self-command, "What your majesty does me the honor to say to me would be very painful to hear were I of an age to be afflicted by it."

Once when Napoleon was introduced to a lady whom he was very anxious to meet, he said, "Why, they told me you were very beautiful."

There are many people who do not try to be agreeable to others who do not interest them, and show a deplorable lack of tact. If a person has any little habit or peculiarity which offends them, they do not care to associate with him, and do not hesitate to show their dislike. If forced into the company of a person who does not attract them, they either freeze him with their cold indifference, so as to shut off the intercourse altogether, or they make him feel very uncomfortable in some way.

There is no better discipline in the world than to force ourselves to be sociable and interesting to those for whom we do not care. It is really surprising how much one can find of interest, even in those who at first repel us. It is not difficult for an intelligent, cultivated person to find something of real interest in everyone.

The fact is, our prejudices are often very superficial, based frequently upon an unfortunate first impression, so that we often find that people who repelled us at first, who seemed very unattractive, and not likely to have anything in common with us, finally become our best friends. Knowing this, we ought at least to give another the advantage of a fair trial before we jump to the conclusion that we are not going to like him or her.

We are creatures of prejudice, and we know from experience that even people towards whom we feel kindly often misjudge and do not like us simply because they do not know us. They are prejudiced by some false impression or hasty opinion of us; but when they are better acquainted the prejudice wears off and they can appreciate our good points.

Some writer has thus described the qualities which enter into tact:

"A sympathetic knowledge of human nature, its fears, weaknesses, expectations, and inclinations.

"The ability to put yourself in the other person's place, and to consider the matter as it appears to him.

"The magnanimity to deny expression to such of your thoughts as might unnecessarily offend another.

" The ability to perceive quickly what is the expedient thing, and the willingness to make the necessary concessions.

"The recognition that there are millions of different human opinions, of which your own is but one.

"A spirit of unfeigned kindness such as makes even an enemy a debtor to your innate good-will.

" A recognition of what is customary under the circumstances and a gracious acceptance of the situation.

"Gentleness, cheerfulness, and sincerity."

Some people are color-blind and have not the slightest appreciation of delicate tints .. Many are tact-blind.

"Don't, on any account, allude to the execution that is to take place to-day," said the wife of a tactless man as she and her liege lord were on their way to a luncheon party. " The people of the house are distantly related to Miss H though they don't talk about the cousinship."

All went well as long as the man bore this in mind, but before the visit was over he broke a rather oppressive silence 'by remarking:

"Well, I suppose Miss H has been hanged by now."

When tactful people first meet us they try to find out what we are interested in and talk about that. They do not talk about themselves or what they are doing, for they know that there is nothing which will interest you quite so much as your own affairs, or conversation along the line of your own ambition. On the other hand, tactless people are always talking about what interests themselves and often become breatbores to strangers as well as to their friends.

It is a great art to interest oneself in others, to be able to strike a responsive chord so that you will make a stranger feel at the introduction that there is something in common between you. It is said that the test of a beautiful woman's popularity is that she seems to belong to everybody.

How easy it is to meet tactful people for the first time! No matter how embarrassing or strained the occasion, they put us at ease at once. They make us feel perfectly at home. This is the test of tact; that you can put shy people, timid people, people who have had little experience in the world, at ease at once. Never mind what you know.

Do not try to dazzle others with your great knowledge upon a certain subject. Just try to find out what will interest them, and make them feel comfortable and unrestrained.

7
"I HAD A FRIEND"

Oh, friendship! of all things the most rare, and therefore most scarce because most excellent, whose comforts in misery are always sweet, and whose counsels in prosperity are ever fortunate.-LILLY.

"I HAD a friend!" Is there anything more beautiful in all this world than the consciousness of possessing sweet, loyal, helpful friends, whose devotion is not affected in the least by a for tune or the lack of it; friends who love us even more in adversity than in prosperity?

At the breaking out of the Civil War, when the qualifications of the different candidates for the Presidency were being discussed, and Lincoln was mentioned, someone said: "Lincoln has nothing, only plenty of friends." It is true that Lincoln was poor, that when he was elected to the legislature of his State he borrowed money to buy a suit of clothes, in order that he might make a respectable appearance, and that he walked a hundred miles to take his seat. It is a matter of history that he also borrowed money to move his family to Washington after he was elected President, but how rich was this marvelous man in his friendships!

Friends are silent partners every one of them interested in everything that interests the other, everyone trying to help the other to succeed in life, to make a good impression, to stand for the best thing in him and not the worst, trying to help the other do what he is endeavoring to do, rejoicing in every good thing that comes to him. Can anything be more sublime, more beautiful than the loyalty, the devotion of friends!

Even with all his remarkable ability, Theodore Roosevelt could never have accomplished anything equal to what he has but for the powerful, persistent, enthusiastic assistance of his friends. It is doubtful whether he would ever have been President but for the loyalty of friends, especially of those he made while a student at Harvard University. Hundreds of his classmates and college mates were working hard for him, both while he was candidate for Governor of New York and for President of the United States. The wonderfully enthusiastic friendship of his regiment of

"Rough Riders" came back to him in tens of thousands of votes in the South and West in the Presidential election.

Just think of what it means to have enthusiastic friends always looking out for our interests, working for us all the time, saying a good word for us at every opportunity, supporting us, speaking for us in our absence when we need a friend, shielding our sensitive, weak spots, stopping slanders, killing lies which would injure us, correcting false impressions, trying to set us right, overcoming the prejudices created by some mistake or slip, or a bad first impression we may have made in some silly moment; always doing something to give us a lift or to help us along.

What sorry figures many of us would cut but for our friends! What marred and scarred reputations most of us would have but for the cruel blows that have been warded off by our friends, the healing balm that they have applied to the hurts of the world. Many of us would have been very much poorer financially, too, but for the hosts of friends who sent us customers and clients and business, and who have always turned our way everything they could.

Oh, what a boon our friends are to our weaknesses, our idiosyncrasies and shortcomings, our failures generally. How they throw a mantle of charity over our faults, and cover up our defects!

What is more beautiful than to see a man trying to draw the curtain before the weaknesses or the scars of his friend, to shield him from the harsh criticism of the thoughtless or heartless, to bury his weaknesses in silence, and to proclaim his virtues upon the housetop! We cannot help admiring such a man, because we know that he is a true friend.

Is there anything more sacred in this world than the office of a true friend? How few of us appreciate what it means to have the reputation of another in our keeping! The report we send out, our estimate of another, may have a great deal to do with the success or failure of the individual. The scandal which we allow to pass unchallenged may mar a reputation for life.

One of the most touching things I know of is the office of a real friend to one who is not a friend to himself one who has lost his self-respect, his self-control, and fallen to the level of the brute. Ah! this is friendship, indeed, which will stand by us when we will not stand by ourselves! I know a man who thus stood by a friend who had become such a slave to drink and all sorts of vice that even his family had turned him out-of-doors. Even when father and mother and wife and children had forsaken him, this friend remained loyal. He followed him at night *in* his debauches, and many a time saved him from freezing to death when he was so inebriated that. he could not stand. Scores of times this man left his home and searched in the slums for his friend, to keep him from the hands of a policeman and to shield him from the cold; and this great love and devotion finally redeemed the fallen man and sent him back to decency and to his home. Can' any money measure the value of such devotion!

Oh! what a difference a friend has made in the lives of most of us! How many people a strong loyal friendship has kept from utter despair, from giving up the struggle for success! How many men and women have been kept from suicide by the thought that someone loved them, believed in them; how many have preferred to suffer tortures to dishonoring or disappointing their friends! The thrill of encouragement which has come from the pressure of a friendly hand, or a sympathetic, friendly word, has proved the turning-point in many a life.

Many a man endures hardships and suffers privations and criticism in the hope of winning at last for the sake of his friends, of those who love and believe in him, and who see in him what others do not, when, if he had only himself to consider, he would give up with little effort.

The faith of friends is a perpetual stimulus.

How it nerves and encourages us to do our best, when we feel that scores of friends really believe in us when others misunderstand and denounce us!

"Life is to be fortified by many friendships," said Sydney Smith. "To love and to be loved is the greatest happiness of existence."

Was there ever such capital for starting in business for oneself as plenty of friends? How many people, who are now successful, would have given up the struggle in some great crisis of their lives, but for the encouragement of a friend which tided them over the critical place! How barren and lean our lives would be if stripped of all that our friends have done for us.

If you are starting out in a profession or in business, the reputation of having a lot of stanch friends will give you backing, will bring you patients, clients, customers. It has been said that "destiny is determined by friendship."

It would be interesting and helpful if we could analyze the lives of successful people, and those who have been highly honored by their fellow men, and find out the secret of their success.

I have tried to make this analysis in the case of one man, whose career I have for a long time carefully studied, and I believe that at least twenty per cent. of his success is due to his remarkable ability to make friends. He has cultivated the friendship faculty most assiduously from boyhood, and he fastens people to him so solidly and enthusiastically, that they would do almost anything to please him.

When this man began his career the friend ships formed in school and college were of immense value in helping him to positions which not only opened up unusual opportunities, but added very largely to his reputation as well.

In other words, his natural ability has been multiplied many times by the help of his hosts of friends. He seems to have a peculiar faculty of enlisting their interest, their hearty, enthusiastic support in everything he does, so that they are always trying to advance his interests.

Very few give the credit they ought to their friends. Most successful men think that they have won out because of their great ability, because they have fought and conquered; and they are always boasting of the wonderful things they have done. They attribute their success wholly to their own smartness, their own sagacity and shrewdness, to their push, their progressiveness. They do not realize that scores of friends, like so many unpaid traveling salesmen, have been helping them at every opportunity.

"True friendship," says C. C. Colton, "is like sound health, the value of it is seldom known until it be lost."

The character and standing of your friends will have a very marked influence upon your life. Make it a rule to choose upwards just as far as possible. Try to associate with people who are your superiors, not so much with people who have more money, but with those who have had greater advantages for culture and self-improvement, who are better educated and better informed, in order that you may absorb as much as possible that will help you. This will tend to raise your own ideals, to inspire you to higher things, to make a greater effort to be somebody yourself.

I know young people who have plenty of friends, but they are not the kind that help or elevate them. They have chosen downward, instead of upward.

If you habitually associate with people be low you, they will tend to drag you down, lower your ideals, your ambition.

We little realize what a great molding, fashioning influence our friends and acquaintances have upon us. Every person 'we come in contact with stamps an indelible influence upon us, and the influence will be like his character. If we form a habit of always trying to better our friendships and acquaintances, we unconsciously acquire the habit of perpetual self-betterment, self-improvement, The great thing is to keep the life standards high. An aspiring habit will tend to do this. However, we should not be intolerant and expect too much of our friends.

"Take your friends more as you find them, without the desire to make them live up to some ideal standard of your own," says a writer. "You may find that their own standard, while different, may not be 50 bad, after all."

It is possible to measure up a man we have never seen, by studying his friends. It is possible to tell pretty nearly how much of a man he is, whether he will stand by his word or whether he is unreliable, or treacherous.

Look out for the man who has practically no friends. You will find something wrong in him somewhere. If he was worthy of friends he would have had them.

"To be rich in friends" is not a sentimental expression; it is of real market worth. To the man or woman "rich in friends" doors are opened and opportunities presented that often are not within reach of those merely rich in money, and are never heard of by the woe-begone who live in the depths.

He is poor indeed who has no friends

What wealth would be a substitute for friendships! How many millionaires would give a large part of their wealth to regain the friends they have lost by neglect while they were making their money!

Not half a dozen people outside of his immediate family attended the funeral of a very rich man who died not long since in New York. But a few weeks later a large church was filled to the doors and the streets were rendered impassable by the crowds assembled to pay the last respects to a man who died without leaving even a thousand dollars behind him.

The latter loved his friends as a miser loves his gold. Everybody who knew him seemed to be his friend. He took infinitely more pride in thinking that he was rich in friendships than he could possibly have taken in a fortune. He would divide his last dollar with anyone who needed it. He did not try to sell his services as dearly as possible. He gave himself to his friends gave himself without reserve, royally, generously, magnanimously. There was no stinting of effort or service in this man's life, nothing that ever suggested selfishness or greed. Is it any wonder that thousands of people should regard his death as a great personal loss?

"In friendship," says Seneca, "there must be no reserve; as much deliberation as you please before the league is struck, but no doubtings nor jealousies after. It requires time to consider a friendship, but the resolution once taken entitles him to my very heart. The purpose of friendship is to have one dearer to me than myself, and for the saving of whose life I would gladly lay down my own, taking with me the consciousness that only the wise can be friends; others are mere companions."

It is only he who loses his life, who gives it royally, in kindly, helpful service to others, that finds it. This is the sowing that gives the bountiful harvest. The man who gets all he can and gives nothing, cannot get real riches. He is like the farmer who thinks too much of his seed-corn to sow it and hoards it, thinking he will be richer for the hoarding. He does not give it to the soil because he cannot see the harvest in the seed. It is not so much a question of how far we have gotten along in the world ourselves, as of how many others we have helped to get on.

Perhaps really the richest man who ever lived upon this continent was Abraham Lincoln, because he gave himself to his people. He did not try to sell his ability to the highest bidder. Great fees had no attraction for him. Lincoln lives in history because he thought more of his friends and all his countrymen were his friends than he did of his pocketbook. He gave himself to his country as a farmer gives his seed to the earth, and what a harvest from that sowing. The end of it no man shall see.

64

.One of the saddest phases of our strenuous American life is the terrible slaughter of friendships by our dollar chasers.

Our strenuous, rushing, electric life in this country is not conducive to the formation of real friendships, such as exist in some foreign countries. We do not have time for them. The vast resources and marvelous opportunities tend to develop an abnormal ambition. The great prizes appeal to our selfish natures, to the brute in us, and we rush and drive at such a killing pace that we cannot take time to cultivate friendships, except those which will help us to our goal.

The result is that we Americans have a great many very pleasant acquaintances, helpful acquaintances, acquaintances which pay us well, but we have comparatively few friends in the highest sense of the word.

The fact is that the tremendous material prizes abnormally develop some very undesirable qualities, and stunt and starve many of our most desirable qualities, making us one-sided.

We have developed colossal money glands in our brain for secreting dollars; and, in the process, we have lost that which is invaluable. We have commercialized our friendships, commercialized our ability, our energy, our time. Everything possible has been turned into dollars; and the result is that we have money, but many of us have not much else.

Thousands of rich men are nobodies outside of their own little business ruts. They have not developed enough of their higher brain cells, not enough of the better part of themselves to rank as high-class men. They are first-class money makers, second or third class in everything else. They have cashed in everything their friendships, their influence, their life-work everything into dollars.

Is there anything more chilling in this world than to have a lot of money but practically no friends? What does that thing which we call success amount to if we have sacrificed our friendships, if we have sacrificed the most sacred things in life in getting it? We may have plenty of acquaintances, but acquaintances are not friends. There are plenty of rich people in this country to-day who scarcely know the luxury of real friendship.

There is something that is called friendship which follows us as long as we are prosperous and have anything to give of money or influence, but which forsakes us when we are down. "True friendship," said

Washington, "is a plant of slow growth, and must undergo and withstand the shocks of adversity before it is entitled to the appellation."

I knew a man who once thought he was unusually rich in real friendships, but, when he lost his money and with it much of his influence, those who were apparently devoted to him before forsook him, and the poor man was so distressed and disappointed over their disaffection that he nearly lost his mental balance.

But a few real friends clung to him in his adversity. When his home and his large business were gone, two of his old servants drew every penny they had out of the savings-bank and insisted upon his taking it to help him to start again. An engineer who used to work for him also remained loyal in adversity and loaned him every cent he had. Through the devotion of those true friends, this man soon recovered his standing and in a comparatively short time became rich again.

Never trust people who trade on friendship, who use it as their greatest asset; people who see capital in your friendship because they can use you to their own advantage. There never was a time when so many used their friends for personal gain as now.

He who prizes his friends should be very careful about his business transactions with them, and especially careful about borrowing money from them. It is a remarkable trait of human nature that some people will do almost anything for us, and we can ask almost any favor of them without losing their confidence or friendship, except that of loaning us money.

How many of us regret the day that we asked a friend for a loan, for, even when it was freely granted, there was not always quite the same feeling afterwards. Some people can never loan others money without having a sort of contempt for them ever afterwards. This ought not to be so, but it is. There are people who will forgive almost anything except a request for money or material assistance. Somehow this is not compatible with the average friendship. You say that real friendship would not be so easily forfeited, but unfortunately most of us have had a sad experience along this line. We may have gotten the money or the help, but a little estrangement, a strained relation between us and our friend, has resulted.

There is a new kind of friendship which is coming more and more into vogue; and that is, business friendship, the friendship that means pecuniary gain. It is a dangerous friendship because of the selfish motive. It is dangerous because it simulates the genuine so nearly that it is difficult to distinguish between one's real friends and those who are false.

I know a man who is thoroughly wanting in the capacity for real friendship; and yet he has so assiduously cultivated the friendship of people for business purposes, cultivated it as so much power to be used to further his own ends, that he appears to be friendly to everybody, and a stranger who meets him for the first time often thinks that he has gained a real friend, when he would really sacrifice him at the first opportunity, without the slightest hesitation, if he saw it would be to his advantage.

It is impossible for the man who looks at everything through selfish glasses to be a real friend to anybody.

There are plenty of people in New York and the large cities who make a profession of trading in their friendships. They have that peculiar magnetic power which attracts people quickly and strongly; but all the time they are weaving their little spider's web, and before the victim is aware of it, he finds himself hopelessly immeshed.

One of the most despicable things a man can do is to use others as a ladder to climb to some coveted position, and then, after he has attained it, kick the ladder down.

The habit of cultivating friendships because it pays, because it will increase one's business, one's pull, one's influence, one's credit; because it brings more clients, more patients, more customers, is dangerous, for it tends to kill the real friendship faculties.

What a delightful, delicious thing it is to have friends who love us for our own sake, who have no " axes to grind," who are always ready to make any sacrifice of comfort, of time, or money when we are in need!

Cicero said that man had received nothing better from the immortal gods, nothing more delightful than friendship. But friendship must be cultivated. It cannot be bought; it is priceless. If you abandon your friends for a quarter of a century or more while you are buried in your pursuit of wealth, you cannot expect to go back and find them where you left them. Did you ever get or keep anything worthwhile without an effort equal to its value?

Only he has friends worthwhile who is willing to pay the price for making and keeping them. He may not have quite as large a fortune as if he gave all of his time to money making. But wouldn't you rather have more good, stanch friends who believe in you, and who would stand by you in the severest adversity, than have a little more money? What will enrich the life so much as hosts of good loyal friends?

Many people seem to think that friendship is a one-sided affair. They enjoy their friends, enjoy having them come to see them, but they rarely think of putting themselves out to reciprocate, or take the trouble to keep up their friendships, while the fact is, reciprocation is the very essence of friendship.

It does not matter how much knowledge you have or what your accomplishments are, you will live a cold, friendless, isolated life and will be unattractive, unless you have come in close constant contact with other lives, unless you have cultivated your sympathies and have taken a real interest in others, have suffered with them, rejoiced with them, helped them.

I am acquainted with a young man who is always complaining that he has no friends, and who says that in his loneliness he sometimes contemplates suicide; but no one who knows him wonders at his isolation, for he possesses qualities which everybody detests. He is closefisted, mean, stingy in money matters, is always criticizing others, is pessimistic, lacks charity and magnanimity, is full of prejudice, is utterly selfish and greedy, is always questioning people's motives when they do a generous act, and yet he wonders why he does not have friends.

If you would have friends, you must cultivate the qualities which you admire in others. Strong friendships rest upon a social, generous, hearty nature. There is nothing like magnanimity and real charity, kindness, and a spirit of helpfulness, for attracting others. Your interest in people must be a real one, or you will not draw them to you.

No great friendship can rest. upon pretense or deception, Opposite qualities cannot attract each other. After all, friendship rests largely upon admiration. There must be something worthy in you, something lovable, before anybody will love you.

Many people are not capable of forming great friendships because they do not have the qualities themselves which attract noble qualities in others. If you are chock-full of despicable qualities, you cannot expect anyone to care for you.

If you are uncharitable, intolerant, if you lack generosity, cordiality, if you are narrow and bigoted, unsympathetic, small, and mean, you cannot expect that generous, large-hearted, noble characters will flock around you. If you expect to make friends with large-souled, noble characters you must cultivate large-heartedness, generosity, and tolerance. One reason why so many people have so few friends is that they have so little to give, and they expect so much. A happy temperament, a desire to scatter joy and gladness, to be helpful to everybody with whom one comes in contact, are wonderful aids to friendship.

You will be amazed to see how quickly friends will flock about you just as soon as you begin to cultivate attractable and lovable qualities.

Justice and truth are absolutely essential to the highest friendship, and we respect a friend all the more because he is just and true, even when it hurts and mortifies us most. We cannot help respecting justice and truth because we are built on these lines; they are a part of our very nature. The friendship which shrinks from telling the truth, which cannot bear to pain one when justice demands it, does not command as high a quality of admiration as the friendship which is absolutely just and truthful.

There is something inherent in human nature which makes us despise the hypocrite.

'We may overlook a weakness in a friend, which makes it hard for him to be absolutely truthful, but if we ever detect him trying to deceive us, we never have quite the same confidence in him again, and confidence is the very basis of real friendship.

"Friendship carries with it love. The true friend is not one made in a hurry. There is no friend like the old one with whom you went bird nesting in your youth, the friend that has plodded along life's road with you shoulder to shoulder.

"When you have a friend who has proven himself such, never let up So long as you live in your evidences of gratitude for the kindness he has shown you. Repay him with interest for his good offices, and let your actions towards him ever be a source of happiness and pleasure to him.

"Nothing is so much appreciated between friends as gratitude, and nothing will kill friendship like ingratitude.

"Genuine friendship is such a rare jewel that when you have a positive demonstration of it, let it be your great concern that you will do nothing to mar this friendship, for broken friendship is a source of grief to both friends so long as they live."

The friendships that last rest more upon a solid respect, admiration, and great congeniality than upon a passionate love. Where the love is so great that it defeats justice and truth, friends are more likely to fall out. The strongest, the most lasting, devoted friendships are those which are based upon principle, upon respect, admiration, and esteem.

"I would go to hell, if there were such a place, with any friend of mine, and I would want no heaven of which I have ever read if any friend of mine were in the outer dark," was the startling assertion of the Rev. Minot J. Savage, in the course of a sermon on "The Companionship of Friends."

"False friends are like our shadows, keeping close to us while we walk in the sunshine, but leaving us the instant we cross into the shade," says Bovee.

Real friendship will follow us into the shadows, into the dark as well as into the sunshine.

The capacity for friendship is a great test of character. We instinctively believe in people who are known to stick to their friends through thick and thin. It is an indication of the possession of splendid qualities. You can generally trust a man who never goes back on a friend. People who lack loyalty have no capacity for great friendship.

After all, isn't a man's success best measured by the number and quality of his friendships? For, no matter how much money he may have accumulated, if he doesn't have a lot of friends there is certainly some tremendous lack in him somewhere, a great lack of sterling qualities. Children ought to, be taught that the most sacred thing in this world is a true friend, and they ought to be trained to cultivate a capacity for friendships. This would broaden their characters, develop fine qualities, and sweeten their lives as nothing else could.

One of the most beautiful things that can ever be said of a human being is that he has a host of loyal, true friends. "No man is useless," said Robert Louis Stevenson, " while he has a friend."

8
AMBITION

"The youth who does not look up will look down, and the spirit that does not soar is destined to grovel."

"Whoever is satisfied with what he does has reached his culminating point. He will progress no more."

IT is astonishing how many people there are who have no definite aim or ambition, but just exist from one day to another with no well-defined life plan. All about us on the ocean of life we see young men and women aimlessly drifting without rudder or port, throwing away time, without serious purpose or method in anything they do. They simply drift with the tide. If you ask one of them what he is going to do,· what his ambition is, he will tell you he does not exactly know yet what he will do. He is simply waiting for a chance to take up something.

How can a man who lives without a pro gram ever expect to arrive anywhere but in chaos, confusion? A clear-cut purpose has a powerful influence upon the life. It unifies our efforts and gives direction to our work, so that every blow counts.

I have never known anyone who followed an indolent inclination ever to amount to much. It is the man who struggles against the things that are fighting with his ambition who gets to the front.

No one ever amounts to much who does not take himself in hand and force himself to do the thing that is best for him in the end, not the pleasantest or the easiest.

Every man should be a stern schoolmaster to himself. He cannot sit and take it easy every time he has the opportunity; he cannot lie abed until he feels like getting up in the morning, and work only when he is in the mood, and ever amount to anything. He must learn to master his moods and to force himself to work no matter how he feels.

Most of the ambitionless people who fail are too lazy to succeed. They are not willing to put themselves out, to pay the price, to make the necessary effort. They want to have a good time. Why should they struggle and strive and strain? Why not enjoy life, take it easy?

Physical laziness, mental indifference, an inclination to let things slide, to go along the line of the least resistance, these are the causes which have made up the great failure army.

One of the first symptoms of deterioration in one's work is the gradual, unconscious oozing out, shrinkage, of one's ambition. There is no one quality in our lives that requires more careful watching and constant bracing up, jacking up, so to speak, than our ambition, especially when we do not keep in an atmosphere which tends to arouse one to life's possibilities.

The habit of watching the ambition constantly and keeping it awake, is absolutely imperative to those who would keep from deteriorating. Everything depends on the ambition. The moment it becomes weak all the life standards drop with it. One must keep the ambition lamp ever-trimmed and burning brightly.

It is dangerous to dally with ambition-killing influences.

When a person has taken an overdose of morphine, a doctor knows that sleep would be fatal, and every effort is made to keep the patient awake. He is sometimes obliged to resort to what seems to be most cruel treatment, pinching and pounding the patient, to keep off that slumber from which there would be no awakening. So it is with ambition; if it once goes to sleep, it is almost impossible to arouse it.

Everywhere we see human watches with splendid equipment, apparently all ready to run, and we wonder why they are silent, why they do not keep good time. The reason is, they have no mainspring, no ambition. '

A watch may have perfect wheels, it may have a very costly jeweled setting, but if it lacks a mainspring, it is useless. So a youth may have a college education, excellent health, but if he lacks ambition, all his other equipments, no matter how superb, will not amount to much.

I know capable men more than thirty years of age who have not yet chosen their lift-work. They say they do not know for what they are fitted.

Ambition often begins very early to knock for recognition. If we do not heed its voice, if it gets no encouragement after appealing to us for years, it gradually ceases to trouble us, because, like any other unused quality or function, it deteriorates or disappears when unused.

Nature allows us to keep only that which is in constant use. The moment we stop exercising muscle, brain, or faculty, deterioration sets in, and the power 'is taken away from us.

If you do not heed the early call of "Upward!" if you do not encourage and nourish your ambition, and constantly strengthen it by vigorous exercise, it will soon die.

An unfed ambition is like a postponed resolution. Its demand for recognition becomes less and less imperious, just as the constant denying of any desire or passion tends to its extinction.

All about us we see people in whom ambition has died. They have the appearance of human beings, but the fire that was once in them has gone out. They walk the earth, but they barely exist. Their usefulness is gone. They are of no account to themselves or the world.

If there is a pitiable sight in the world, it is a person in whom ambition is dead, the man who has denied and denied that inward voice which bids him up and on, the man in whom ambition's fires have cooled from the lack of fuel.

There is always hope for a person, no matter how bad he is, as long as his ambition is alive; but when that is dead beyond resuscitation, the great life-spur, the impelling motive is gone.

One of the most difficult things a human being can do is to keep his ambition from fading out, his aspirations sharp and fresh, his ideals clear and clean-cut.

Many deceive themselves into thinking that if they keep aspiring, if they keep longing to carry out their ideals, to reach their ambition, they are actually realizing their dreams. But there is such a thing as aspiring too much, as forming the dreaming habit to one's injury.

Ambition requires a great deal and a great variety of food to keep it vigorous. A namby-pamby ambition does not amount to anything. It must be backed by a robust will power, stern resolve, physical energy, powers of endurance, to be effective.

The fact that you have an almost uncontrollable impulse, a great absorbing ambition to do a thing which meets with the approval of your judgment and your better self, is a notice served upon you that you can do the thing, and should do it at once.

Some people seem to think that the ambition to do a certain thing in life is a permanent quality which will remain with them. It is not. It is like the daily manna which fell for the daily needs of the Israelites in the desert. They had to use it at once. When their faith was weak they tried to store it up, but they found it would never keep until the next day.

The time to do a thing is when the spirit is upon us, when it makes a sharp, clean-cut impression upon us. Resolution fades and becomes dimmer at every postponement. When the desire, the ambition, comes fresh and strong with zeal and enthusiasm, it is easy; but after we have postponed it a few times, we find ourselves less 'and less inclined to make the necessary effort or sacrifice to attain it, because it does not appeal to us with the same emphasis as at first.

Do not allow the ambition to cool. Make up your mind that you cannot and will not spend your life being half satisfied. Rouse your spirit, and go toward the goal which is worthwhile.

It is one of the most discouraging problems in the world to try to help the ambitionless, the half satisfied, those who have not discontent enough in their natures to push them on, initiative enough to begin things, and persistency enough to keep going.

You cannot do much with a young man who is apparently contented to drift along in a humdrum way, half content with his accomplishments, undisturbed by the fact that he has used but a very small part of himself, a very small percentage of his real ability, that his energies are running to waste in all sorts of ways. You cannot do much with a young man who lacks ambition, life, energy, and vigor, who is willing to slide along the line of the least resistance, and who exerts himself as little as possible. There is nothing upon which to build. Even those foundations which he had at the start are slowly crumbling to uselessness.

It is the young man who is not satisfied with what he does, and who is determined to better it every day, who struggles to express the ideal, to make the possible in him a reality.

The trouble with many men is that their ideals are too low, too common, too dull. They do not keep their hope bright or aspire enough. They live in their animal senses. We must aspire if we would rise. We cannot climb while looking down. The ambition must always precede the achievement. The higher civilization climbs, the higher the ambition; the higher the ambition, the finer the people.

What would become of the human race if everyone had reached his goal; had attained his ambition? Would anyone want to work anymore than he felt like working? Who would do all the drudgery?

Suppose everyone was in the condition of the sons and daughters of many rich parents whose sole object is to have a good time, to enjoy all the pleasant things, and to avoid all of the work and disagreeable experience possible. How long would it take a world so peopled to retrograde to barbarism?

The struggle of man to rise a little higher, to get into a little more comfortable position, to secure a little better education, a little better home, to gain a little more culture and refinement, to possess that power which comes from being in a position of broader and wider influence through the acquirement of property, is what has developed the character and the stamina of our highest types of manhood today. This upward life-trend gives others confidence in us.

Ambition is the Moses that has led the human race through the wilderness and into sight of the promised land, the millennium. It is true that vast multitudes of human beings are still following far in the rear, so far that it would seem almost impossible for them ever to get a glimpse of the land of promise, but still there is an improvement even in the semi-civilized.

The quality of the ambitions of a people at any time locates them in the scale of civilization. The ideals of an individual or a nation measure the actual condition and the future possibilities and probabilities.

One of the most hopeful signs in our civilization to-day is the evolution in ideals.

In every department of life our ideals or ambition are becoming higher, purer, cleaner. Our march of progress and improvement is so rapid that it requires a greater ambition, loftier ideals, a higher order of intellect, and stronger effort for achievement in every line of endeavor than formerly.

The ideals are gradually leavening the whole human mass, and will ultimately bring every human being into his own, into that state of blessedness which is undoubtedly his birthright.

It is only the man who has stopped growing that feels satisfied with his achievements. The growing man feels a great lack of wholeness, of completeness, Everything in him seems to be unfinished because it is growing. The expanding man is always dissatisfied with his accomplishment, is always reaching out for something larger, fuller, completer.

Nothing else contributes to one's advancement in life as the formation of the climbing habit in everything, the perpetual ambition and effort to do a little better to-day than yesterday, to do everything we attempt a little better than we have done it in the past.

It is a wonderful aid to growth to associate constantly with people who are above us, who are better educated, more cultivated, more refined, who have had rich experience in lines of which we know little. We all know how quickly one deteriorates when all his tendencies are downward, when he seeks the company of those below him, and common, demoralizing pleasures. When this process is reversed, the upward tendency, the upward progress, is equally as pronounced.

The lofty aspiration habit becomes a great uplifting force in any life. It broadens all the mental faculties and arouses new powers, new possibilities in the sub-consciousness which would never respond to the ordinary ambition or sordid motive. It awakens the Great Within, arouses the resourcefulness in the subconscious nature which would remain dormant under ordinary conditions.

No one can do anything very great unless he is spurred on by an ambition which takes the drudgery out of his task, an enthusiasm which lightens his burdens and cheers the way. The man who goes to his work as a galley-slave to his oar, as a tired horse to his load too heavy to pull, can never accomplish much; there must be a zeal and great ambition and love for the work, or either mediocrity or failure must result.

It is a very difficult thing to succeed in life under the most favorable conditions, but to love your work is a tremendous help; a great tonic. Enthusiasm seems to make us unconscious of danger and obstacles. If you find your ambition dying out, if you do not feel the old zeal for your work, if you are not so interested that you long to go to it in the morning and hate to leave it at night, there is something wrong somewhere. Perhaps you have not found your right place; discouragement may have killed your enthusiasm and diminished your zest; but, whatever the cause of your lowering standard, if you find your ambition on the decline, if you find it harassing to go to your task, if you feel the drudgery of your work increasing, do everything **to** remedy it.

It is not difficult to increase enthusiasm, to spur on a lagging ambition, if you set about it as you do about the task you are determined to accomplish. You cannot keep up your friendships without constant cultivation, and the same thing is true of your ambition.

Everywhere we see people side-tracked with their fires banked, the water in their boilers cooled down, and yet they are wondering why express trains fly past them, while they creep along like snails. They fail to remember that banked fires and lukewarm water will not pull their trains at express speed.

These people never renew their rails, do not keep the water in their engines at the boiling point, yet they complain if they fail to reach their destination. They cannot understand why they are so much slower than their neighbor, who flies rapidly past them on perfectly ballasted roads, and with up-to-date engines and cars. If they run off their wretched tracks, they attribute it to hard luck.

The great majority of people who do not amount to anything in the world, those who are sidetracked the idle, the indolent, the mediocre have failed from the lack of ambition.

The youth who hungers for an education, who longs for improvement, no matter how poor, generally finds a way. But there is little hope for the ambitionless; there is no way' of firing, of stirring up, of stimulating those who lack the inclination or ambition to get on in the world.

It is not an easy matter to keep back a boy with an ambition to do something and to be somebody in the world. No matter what his surroundings, no matter how badly he is handicapped, he will find a way out, he will forge ahead. You could not keep back a Lincoln, a Wilson, or a Greeley; if too poor to buy books, they would borrow them and pick up an education.

We need never despair of a youth, no matter how dull or stupid, who has a taste for some thing better.

You may think your life very commonplace, your opportunity of amounting to much very small, but it does not matter how humble your position or what you are doing, if you have a taste for something better, if there is an out-reach and an up-reach in your life, if you aspire to something higher and are willing to pay the price for advancement in downright hard work, you will succeed. You will rise out of your commonness just as surely as the germ, struggling up through the sod, will reach the surface, by persistent pushing.

We should not judge a person by what he is doing, for it may be just a stepping-stone to something higher up, further on. Judge him by what he is ambitious and determined to do. An honest man will do any respectable work as a stepping-stone to his goal.

There is something in the atmosphere of every person which predicts his future; for the way he does things, the energy, the degree of enterprise which he puts into his work, his manner, everything is a telltale of what is awaiting him.

"If you are only swabbing a deck, swab it as if old Davy Jones were after you," says Dickens.

A man may be very dissatisfied with what he is doing without having the aspiration for something higher and the stamina to reach his aim. Mere dissatisfaction with one's position does not always indicate ambition. It may indicate laziness, indifference.

But when we see a man filling a position just as well as it can be filled, trying to do everything to a complete finish, taking great pride in it, and yet having a great longing for something higher and better, we feel certain he will attain it. We cannot tell much about a man until we know what his ambition is. This, if he has grit, persistency, and application, will readily locate him on the human scale.

When young Franklin was struggling to get a foothold in Philadelphia, shrewd business men there predicted, even when he was eating, sleeping, and printing in one room, that he had a great future before him, because he was working with all his might to get up higher, and he carried himself in a way that gave confidence. Everything he did was done so well, with such ability, that it was a prediction of very much larger things. When he was only a journeyman printer he did his work so much better than others, and his system was so much superior even to his employer's that people predicted he would someday have the business which went to that firm, which he did.

Many people who live in remote country districts do not come in contact with standards by which they can measure and compare their own powers. They live a quiet, uneventful life, and there is little in their environment to arouse the faculties which are not active in their vocation.

The ambition of the boy who has lived on a farm in the back country is often aroused the first time he goes to the city. To him the city is a colossal world's fair, where everybody's achievement is on exhibition. The progressive spirit which pervades the city is like an electric shock to him and arouses all of his latent energies, calls out his reserves. Everything he sees seems to be a call to him to go forward, to push on.

This is one advantage of city life, and of travel, coming in contact with others constantly gives us an opportunity to compare ourselves with others, to measure our ability with theirs. There is the contagion of example which tends to arouse and prod. The contact with others helps to arouse the love of conquest, the passion to try our strength with others.

Then, in the city or in traveling, we are constantly reminded of what others have done. We see the tremendous engineering feats, great factories and offices, vast businesses, all huge advertisers of man's achievement. All these things fill an ambitious youth with interrogation points, and he is always wondering why he does not do something himself. And when he wants to do it, when he longs to do a thing and believes he can, his power is multiplied.

Men often fail because of an impatient ambition. They cannot wait to prepare for their life-work, but think they must leap into a position which others have been years in reaching. They are over-ambitious,' impatient of results, and have no time to do anything properly. Everything is hurried and forced. Such people do not develop symmetrically, but are one-sided, lacking judgment and good sense.

"The heights by great men reached and kept
Were not attained by sudden flight,
But they, while their companions slept,
Were toiling upward in the night."

We frequently see sad examples of unbridled ambition men who have been spurred on by an overvaulting ambition, men whose sensibilities have been so benumbed by the ambition to become rich or powerful, that they have stooped to do very questionable things. Ambition often blinds one to justice.

There is nothing more pitiable than to see a man the victim of an inordinate, selfish ambition to advance himself at all costs, to gain fame, or notoriety, no matter who is sacrificed in the process.

It is very difficult to see the right, to get a clear perspective of justice, when we become victims of an overvaulting ambition. Men so intoxicated have stopped at no crime. Napoleon and Alexander the Great are good examples of the wrecks which an unbridled ambition makes of its victims.

"""Just an ambition to excel may become a very dangerous force, and may lead to all sorts of sacrifices of character.

"Everyone should have an ambition to do something distinctive, something individual, something which will take him out of mediocrity, which will lift him above the ambitionless, the energyless. It is perfectly proper to be ambitious to get up as high in the world as possible, and this we may do with all charity and kindliness of heart toward our neighbors.

The fellow who must be aroused is yourself, and every man is entitled to draw his inspiration from whatever source is at hand.

Sometimes the conversation or encouragement of an inspiring man or woman in whom we have great confidence, the faith of someone who believes in us when others do not, who sees something in us which others do not see, arouses the ambition and gives us a glimpse of our possibilities. We may not think much about this at the time, but it may be a turning point in our career.

Multitudes of men and women have caught the first glimpse of themselves by the reading of some inspiring book or some vigorous article. Without it, they might have remained ignorant of their real power forever. Anything that will give us a glimpse of ourselves, that will awaken us to our possibilities, is invaluable.

Choose for your friends those who stimulate you, who arouse your ambition, who stir you up with a desire to do something and to be somebody in the world. One such friend is worth a dozen passive or indifferent friends.

Get close to people who arouse your ambition, who get hold of you, who make you think and feel. Keep close to people who are a perpetual inspiration to you. The great trouble with most of us is that we never get aroused, never discover ourselves until late in life, often too late to make much out of the remnant that is left. It is very important that we become aroused to our possibilities when young, that we may get the greatest possible efficiency out of our lives.

Most people die with the largest percentage **of** their possibilities still undeveloped. They have improved little patches of their ability here and there, while the great estate of their possible selves is untilled, with great mines of wealth untouched.

We cannot use what we do not first discover or see. There are tens of thousands of day laborers in this country -common workmen putting their lives in drudgery, who, if they had only been arouse, would have been employers themselves, w o uld have been men of force, of standing *in* their community, but they have been held down by their ignorance of their own power. They have never discovered themselves, and so they must be "hewers of wood and drawers of water." We see them everywhere, splendid men and women, who impress us as giants in possibility, but who are totally ignorant of the great forces that are sleeping within them.

There are thousands of girls who are spending their lives as clerks or operatives, or in ordinary situations, who, if they could but discover themselves and once see their possibilities, might improve their condition immeasurably and become great living forces in the world.

Sit down and take an inventory of yourself. If you are dissatisfied with what you are doing and think you ought to do better, try to discover, no matter how long it takes you, just where your trouble lies. Find out the things that keep you back. Make long searching tours of discovery in your own consciousness. Say to yourself over and over again, "Why can others do such remarkable things while I do ordinary, common things? Constantly ask yourself, "If others can do them, why cannot I?"

You may find some great nuggets of gold in these tours of self-discovery, which you never dreamed you possessed, great possibilities of power which you never uncovered before, and which may, if developed, revolutionize your life.

One of the fatal dangers of remaining a long time in one position, as a clerk, for example, is that habit tends to make slaves of us. What we did yesterday we are more likely to do to-day; and if we do it to-day, it is still more certain that we will do it to-morrow; and, after a while, using the same faculties in a dry routine, the other, unused faculties begin to wane, grow weaker, atrophy, until we begin to think that what we are doing is the only thing we can do.

What we use becomes stronger; what we do not use weaker; and we are likely to deceive ourselves in underrating the powers we really possess.

Low aim is' crime because it pulls down every other quality to its level. Low aim destroys the executive ability. The faculties and the entire man follow the aim. We must climb, or we must go down. There is no such thing as clinging forever upon one rung of Life's great ladder.

9
EDUCATION BY READING

Books are the windows through which the soul looks out.-H. W. BEECHER.

"TUMBLING around in a library" was the phrase Oliver Wendell Holmes used in describing in part his felicities in boyhood. One of the most important things that wise students get out of their schooldays is a familiarity with books in various departments of learning. The ability to pick out from a library what will be most helpful in life is of the greatest value. It is like a man selecting his tools for intellectual expansion and social service. "Men in every department of practical life," says President Hadley of Yale, "men in commerce, in transportation, or in manufactures, have told me that what they really wanted from our colleges was men who have this selective power of using books efficiently. The beginnings of this kind of knowledge are best learned in any home fairly well furnished with books."

Libraries are no longer a luxury, but a necessity. A home without books and periodicals and newspapers is like a house without windows. Children learn to read by being in the midst of books; they unconsciously absorb knowledge by handling them. No family can now afford to be without good reading.

It is related that Henry Clay's mother furnished him with books by her own earnings at the washtub.

Children who are well supplied with dictionaries, encyclopedias, histories, works of reference, and other useful books, will educate themselves unconsciously and almost without expense, and will learn many things of their own accord in moments which would otherwise be wasted; and which, if learned in schools, academies, or colleges, would cost ten times as much as the expense of the books would be. Besides, homes are brightened and made attractive by good books, and children stay in such pleasant homes; while those whose education has been neglected are anxious to get away from home, drift off, and fall into all manner of snares and dangers.

It is splendid for children to be brought up in the atmosphere of books, and it is astonishing how much a bright child will absorb from good books, if allowed to use them constantly, to handle them, to be familiar with their bindings and titles.

Many people never make a mark on a book, never bend down a leaf, or underscore a choice passage. Their libraries are just as clean as the day they bought them, and often their minds are just about as clean of information. Don't be afraid to mark your books. Make notes in them. They will be all the more valuable. One who learns to use his books in early life grows up with an increasing power for effective usefulness.

Wear threadbare clothes and patched shoes, if necessary, but do not pinch or economize on books. If you cannot give your children an academic education, you can place within their reach a few good books which will lift them above their surroundings, into respectability and honor.

Is not one's early home the place where he should get his principal training for life? It is here we form habits which shape our careers, and which cling to us as long as we live. It is here that regular, persistent mental training should fix the life ever after.

I know of pitiable cases where ambitious boys and girls have longed to improve themselves, and yet were prevented from doing so by the pernicious habits prevailing in the home, where everybody else spent the evenings talking and joking, with no effort at self-improvement, no thought of higher ideals, no impulse to read anything better than a cheap, exciting story. The aspiring members of the family were teased and laughed at until they got discouraged and gave up the struggle.

If the younger ones do not want to read or study themselves, they will not let anybody else so inclined do so. Children are naturally mischievous, and like to tease. They are selfish, too, and cannot understand why anyone else should want to go off by himself to read or study when they want him to play.

Were the self-improvement habit once well established in a home, it would become a delight. The young people would look forward to the study hour with as much anticipation as to playing.

I know a New England family in which all the children and the father and mother, by mutual consent, set aside a portion of each evening for study or some form of self-culture. After dinner, they give themselves completely to recreation. They have a regular romp and play, and all the fun possible for an hour. Then when the time comes for study, the entire house becomes so still that you could hear a pin drop. Everyone is in his place reading, writing, studying, or engaged in some form of mental work. No one is allowed to speak or disturb anyone else. If any member of the family is indisposed, or for any reason does not feel like working, he must at least keep quiet and not disturb the others. There is perfect harmony and unity of purpose an ideal condition for study. Everything that would scatter the efforts or cause the mind to wander, all interruptions that would break the continuity of thought, are carefully guarded against. More is gained in one hour of close, uninterrupted study than in two or three broken by many interruptions, or weakened by mind wandering.

Were it possible for every family that squanders precious time to spend an evening in such a home, it would be an inspiration. A bright, alert, intelligent, harmonious atmosphere so pervades a self-improving home that one feels insensibly uplifted and stimulated to better things.

Sometimes the habits of a home are revolutionized by the influence of one resolute youth who declares himself, taking a stand and announcing that, as for himself, he does not propose to be a failure; that he is going to take no chances as to his future. The moment he does this, he stands out in strong contrast with the great mass of young people who are throwing away their opportunities and have not grit and stamina enough to do anything worthwhile.

The very reputation of always trying to improve yourself in every possible way, of being dead in earnest, will attract the attention of everybody who knows you, and you will get many a recommendation for promotion which never comes to those who make no special effort to climb upward.

There is a great deal of time wasted even in the busiest lives, which, if properly organized, might be used to advantage.

Many housewives who are so busy from morning to night that they really believe they have no time for reading books, magazines, or newspapers' would be amazed to find how much they would have if they would more thoroughly systematize their work. Order is a great time saver, and we certainly ought to be able so to adjust our living plan that we can have a fair amount of time for self-improvement, for enlarging life. Yet many people think that their only opportunity for self-improvement depends upon the time left after everything else has been attended to.

What would a business man accomplish if he did not attend to important matters until he had time that was not needed for anything else? The good business man goes to his office in the morning and plunges right into the important work of the day. He knows perfectly well that if he attends to all the outside matters all the details and little things that come up sees everybody that wants to see him, and answers all the questions people want to ask, it will be time to close his office before he gets to his main business.

Most of us manage somehow to find time for the things we love. If one is hungry for knowledge, if one yearns for self-improvement, if one has a taste for reading, he will make the opportunity.

Where the heart is, there is the treasure. Where the ambition is, there is time.

It takes not only resolution but also de termination to set aside unessentials for essentials, things pleasant and agreeable to-day for the things that will prove best for us in the end. There is always temptation to sacrifice future good for present pleasure; to put off reading to a more convenient season, while we enjoy idle amusements or waste the time in gossip or frivolous conversation.

The greatest things of the world have been done by those who systematized their work, organized their time. Men who have left their mark on the world have appreciated the preciousness of time, regarding it as their great quarry.

If you want to develop a delightful form of enjoyment, to cultivate a new pleasure, a new sensation which you have never before experienced, begin to read good books, good periodicals, regularly every day. Do not tire yourself by trying to read a great deal at first. Read a little at a time, but read some every day, no matter how little. If you are faithful you will soon acquire a taste for reading the reading habit; and it will, in time, give you infinite satisfaction, unalloyed pleasure.

In a gymnasium, one often sees lax, listless people, who, instead of pursuing a systematic course of training to develop all the muscles of the body, flit aimlessly from one thing to another, exercising with pulley-weights for a minute or two, taking up dumb-bells and throwing them down, swinging once or twice on parallel bars, and so frittering away time and strength. Far better it would be for such people to stay away from a gymnasium altogether, for their lack of purpose and continuity makes them lose rather than gain muscular energy. A man or woman who would gather strength from gymnastic exercise must set about it systematically and with a will. He must put mind and energy into the work, or else continue to have flabby muscles and an undeveloped body.

The physical gymnasium differs only in kind from the mental one. Thoroughness and system are as necessary in one as in the other. It is not the tasters of books not those who sip here and there, who take up one book after another, turn the leaves listlessly and hurry to the end, who strengthen and develop the mind by reading.

To get the most from your reading you must read with a purpose. To sit down and pick up a book listlessly, with no aim except to pass away time, is demoralizing. It is much as if an employer were to hire a boy, and tell him he could start when he pleased in the morning, work when he felt like it, rest when he wanted to, and quit when he got tired!

Never go to a book you wish to read for a purpose, if you can possibly avoid it, with a tired, jaded mentality. If you do, you will derive nothing from it. Go to it fresh, vigorous, and with active, never passive, faculties. This practise is a splendid and effective cure for mind-wandering, which afflicts so many people, and which is encouraged by the multiplicity of and facility for obtaining reading matter at the present day.

What can give greater satisfaction than reading with a purpose, and that consciousness of a broadening mind that follows it; the consciousness that we are pushing ignorance, bigotry, and whatever clouds the mind and hampers progress a little further away from us?

The kind of reading that counts, that makes mental fiber and stamina, is that upon which the mind is concentrated. One should approach a book with all one's soul intent upon its contents.

Passive reading is even more harmful in its effects than desultory reading. It will not strengthen the brain any more than sitting in a gymnasium will develop the body. The mind remains inactive, in a sort of indolent revery, wandering here and there, without focusing anywhere. Such reading takes the spring and snap out of the mental faculties, weakens the intellect and makes the brain torpid and incapable of grappling with great principles and difficult problems.

What you get out of a book is not necessarily what the author puts into it, but what you bring to it. If the heart does not lead the head, if the thirst for knowledge, the hunger for a broader and deeper culture, are not the motives for reading, you will not get the most out of a book. But, if your thirsty soul drinks in the writer's thought as the parched soil absorbs rain, then your latent possibilities and the potency of your being, like delayed germs and seeds in the soil, will spring forth into new life.

When you read, read as Macaulay did, as Carlyle did, as Lincoln did as did every great man who has profited by his reading with your whole soul absorbed in what you read, with such intense concentration that you will be oblivious of everything else outside of your book.

"Reading furnishes us only with the materials of knowledge," said John Locke; Hit is thinking that makes what we read ours."

In order to get the most out of books, the reader must be a thinker. The mere acquisition of facts is not the acquisition of power.

To fill the mind with knowledge that cannot be made available is like filling our houses with furniture and brio-a-brae until we have no room to move about.

Food does not become physical force, brain, or muscle until it has been thoroughly digested and assimilated, and has become an integral part of the blood, brain, and other tissues. Knowledge does not become power until digested and assimilated by the brain, until it has become a part of the mind itself.

If you wish to become intellectually strong, after reading with the closest attention, form this habit: frequently close your book and sit and think, or stand and walk and think but think, contemplate, reflect. Turn what you have read over and over in your mind.

It is not yours until you have assimilated it by your thought, taken it into your life. When you first read it, it belongs to the author. It is yours only when it becomes an integral part of you.

Many people have an idea that if they keep reading everlastingly, if they have a book in their hands during every leisure moment, they will, of necessity, become full-rounded and well-educated. This is a mistake. They might just as well expect to become athletes by eating at every opportunity. It is even more necessary to think than to read. Thinking, contemplating what we have read, is what digestion and assimilation are to the food.

Some of the biggest numskulls I know are always cramming themselves with knowledge, everlastingly reading. But they never think. When they get a few minutes' leisure they snatch a book and go to reading. In other words, they are always eating intellectually, but never digesting their knowledge or assimilating it.

I know a young man who has formed such a habit of reading that he is almost never without a book, a magazine, or a paper. He is always reading, at home, on the cars, at the railway stations, and he has acquired a vast amount of knowledge. He has a perfect passion for knowledge, and yet his mind seems to have been weakened by this perpetual brain cramming.

By every reader let Milton's words be borne in mind:

Who reads Incessantly, and to his reading brings not
A spirit and judgment equal or superior,
Uncertain and unsettled still remains,
Deep versed in books and shallow in himself,
Crude or intoxicate, collecting toys
And trifles for choice matters, worth a sponge,
As children gathering pebbles on the shore.

When Webster was a boy, books were scarce, and so precious that he never dreamed that they were to be read only once, but thought they ought to be committed to memory, or read and re-read until they became a part of his very life.

Elizabeth Barrett Browning says, "We err by reading too much, and out of proportion to what we think. I should be wiser, I am persuaded, if

I had not read half as much; should have had stronger and better exercised faculties, and should stand higher in my own appreciation."

People who live more quietly do not have so many distracting influences as others, and consequently they think more deeply and reflect more. They do not read so much but they are better readers.

You should bring your mind to the reading of a book, or to the study of any subject, as you take an ax to the grindstone; not for what you get from the stone, but for the sharpening of the ax.

The greatest advantage of books does not always come under what we remember of them, but from their suggestiveness, their character-building power.

"It is not in the library, but in yourself," says Fr. Gregory, "in your self-respect and your consciousness of duty nobly done-that you are to find the 'Fountain of Youth,' the , Elixir of Life,' and all the other things that tend to preserve life's freshness and bloom. " It is a grand thing to read a good book it is a grander thing to live a good life and in the living of such life is generated the power that defies age and its decadence."

It is not the ability, the education, the knowledge that one has that makes the difference between men. The mere possession of knowledge is not always the possession of power; knowledge, which has not become a part of yourself, knowledge which cannot swing into line in an emergency is of little use, and will not save you at the critical moment.

To be effective, a man's education must become a part of himself as he goes along. *All of it must be worked up into power.* A little practical education that has become a part of one's being and is always available, will accomplish more in the world than knowledge far more extensive that cannot be utilized.

No one better illustrates what books will do for a man, and what a thinker will do with his books, than Gladstone, who was always far greater than his career. He rose above Parliament, reached out beyond politics, and was always growing. He had a passion for intellectual expansion. His peculiar gifts undoubtedly fitted him for the church, or he would have made a good professor at Oxford or Cambridge, but circumstances led him into the political arena, and he adapted himself readily to his environment. He was an all-round well-read man, who thought his way through libraries and through life.

One great benefit of a taste for reading and access to the book world, is the service it renders as a diversion and a solace.

What a great thing to be able to get away from ourselves, to fly away from the harassing, humiliating, discouraging, depressing things about us, to go at will to a world of beauty, joy, and gladness!

If a person is discouraged or depressed by any great bereavement or suffering, the quickest and the most effective way of restoring the mind to its perfect balance, to its normal condition, is to immerse it in a sane atmosphere, an uplifting, encouraging, inspiring atmosphere, and this may always be readily found in the best books.' I have known people who were suffering under the most painful mental anguish, from losses and shocks which almost unbalanced their minds, to be completely revolutionized in their mental state by the suggestive power which came from becoming absorbed in a great book.

Everywhere we see rich old men sitting around the clubs, smoking, looking out of the windows, lounging around hotels, traveling about, uneasy, dissatisfied, not knowing what to do with themselves, because they had never prepared for this part of their lives. They put all their energy, ambition, everything into their vocation.

I know an old gentleman who has been an exceedingly active business man. He has kept his finger upon the pulse of events. He has known what has been going on in the world during his whole active career. And he is now as happy and as contented as a child in his retirement, because he has always been a great reader, a great lover of his kind.

People who keep their minds bent in one direction too long at a time soon lose their elasticity, their mental vigor, freshness, spontaneity.

If I were to quote Mr. Dooley, it would be:

"Reading is not thinking; reading is the next thing this side of going to bed for resting the mind."

To my own mind, however, I would rather cite that versatile Englishman, Lord Rosebery. In a speech at the opening of a Carnegie library at West Calder, Midlothian, he made a characteristic utterance upon the value of books; saying in substance:

" There is, however, one case in which books are certainly an end in themselves, and that is to refresh and to recruit after fatigue. When the object is to refresh and to exalt, to lose the cares of this world in the world of imagination, then the book is more than a means. It is an end in itself. It refreshes, exalts, and inspires the man. From any work, manual or intellectual, the man with a happy taste for books comes in tired and soured and falls into the arms of some great author, who raises him from the ground and takes him into a new heaven and a new earth, where he forgets his bruises and rests his limbs, and he returns to the world a fresh and happy man."

"Who," asks Professor Atkinson, "can overestimate the value of good books, those strips of thought, as Bacon so finely calls them, voyaging through seas of time, and carrying their precious freight so safely from generation to generation? Here are finest minds giving us the best wisdom of present and past ages; here are the intellects gifted far beyond ours, ready to give us the results of lifetimes of patient thought, imaginations open to the beauty of the universe."

The lover of good books can never be very lonely; and, no matter where he is, he can always fine pleasant and profitable occupation and the best of society when he quits work.

Who can ever be grateful enough for the art of printing; grateful enough to the famous authors who have put their best thoughts where we can enjoy them at will? There are some advantages of intercourse with great minds through their books over meeting them in person. The best of them lives in their books, while their disagreeable peculiarities, their idiosyncrasies, their objectionable traits are eliminated. **In** their books we find the authors at their best. Their thoughts are selected, winnowed in their books. Book friends are always at our service, never annoy us, rasp or nettle us. No matter how nervous, tired, or discouraged we may be, they are always soothing, stimulating, uplifting.

We may call up the greatest writer in the middle of the night when we cannot sleep, and he is just as glad to be with us, as at any other time. We are not excluded from any nook or corner in the great literary world; we can visit the most celebrated people that ever lived without an appointment, without influence, without the necessity of dressing or of observing any rules of etiquette. We can drop in upon a Milton, a Shakespeare, an Emerson, a Longfellow, a Whittier without a moment's notice and receive the warmest welcome.

"You get into society, in the widest sense," says Geikie, " in a great library, with the huge advantage of needing no introduction, and not dreading repulses. From that great crowd you can choose what companions you please, for in the silent levees of the immortals there is no pride, but the highest is at the service of the lowest, with a grand humility. You may speak freely with any, without a thought of your inferiority; for books are perfectly well bred, and hurt no one's feelings by any discriminations."

"It is not the number of books," says Professor William Mathews, "which a young man reads that makes him intelligent and well informed, but the number of well-chosen ones that he has mastered, so that every valuable thought in them is a familiar friend."

It is only when books have been read and reread with ever deepening delight that they are clasped to the heart, and become what Macaulay found them to be, the old friends who are never found with new faces, who are the same to us in our wealth and in our poverty, in our glory and in our obscurity. No one gets into the inmost heart of a beautiful poem, a great history, a book of delicate humor, or a volume of exquisite essays, by reading it once or twice. He must have its precious thoughts and illustrations stored in the treasure-house of memory, and brood over them in the hours of leisure.

"A book may be a perpetual companion. Friends come and go, but the book may beguile all experiences and enchant all hours."

"The first time," says Goldsmith, "that I read an excellent book, it is to me just as if I had gained a new friend; when I read over a book I have perused before, it resembles the meeting with an old one."

" No matter how poor I am," says William Ellery Channing, " no matter though the prosperous of my own time will not enter my obscure dwelling; if the sacred writers **will** enter and take up their abode under my roof if Milton will cross my threshold to sing to me of Paradise; and Shakespeare to open to me the worlds of imagination and the workings of the human heart, I shall not pine for want of intellectual companionship, though excluded from what is called the best society in the place where I live." .

"Books," says Milton, "do preserve as in a violl, the purest efficacy and extraction of that living intellect that bred them. A good Book is the pretious life-blood of a master spirit, imbalm'd and treasur'd up on purpose to a Life beyond Life."

"A book is good company," said Henry Ward Beecher. "It comes to your longing with full instruction, but pursues you never. It is not offended at your absent-mindedness, nor jealous if you turn to other pleasures, of leaf, or dress, or mineral, or even of books. It silently serves the soul without recompense, not even for the hire of love. And yet more noble, it seems to pass from itself, and to enter the memory, and to hover in a silvery transformation there, until the outward book is but a body and its soul and spirit are flown to you, and possess your memory like a spirit."

10

DISCRIMINATION IN READING

Cultivate the habit of reading something good for ten minutes a day. Ten minutes a day will in twenty years make all the difference between a cultivated and an uncultivated mind, provided you read what is good. I mean by the good the proved treasures of the world, the intellectual treasures of the world in story, verse, history, and biography. CHARLES W. ELIOT, Ex-President of Harvard University.

FEW books well read, and an intelligent choice of those few,- these are the fundamentals for self-education by reading.

If only a few well chosen, it is better to avail yourself of choices others have already made old books, the standard works tested by many generations of readers. If only a few, let them be books of highest character and established fame. Such books are easily found, even In small public libraries.

It is a cardinal rule that if you do not like a book, do not read it. What another likes, you may not. Any book list is suggestive; it can be binding only on those who prize it. Like attracts like.

Did you ever think that the thing you are looking for is looking for you; that it is the very law of affinities to get together?

If you are coarse in your tastes, vicious in your tendencies, you do not have to work very hard to find coarse, vicious books; they are seeking you by the very law of attraction.

One's taste for reading is much like his taste for food. Dull books are to be avoided, as one refuses food disagreeable to him; to someone else the book may not be dull, nor the food disagreeable. Whole nations may eat cabbage, or stale fish, while I like neither. Ultimately, therefore, every reader must make his own selection, and find the book that finds him. Anyone not a random reader will soon select a short shelf of books that he may like better than a longer shelf that exactly suits someone else. Either will be a shelf of good books and neither a shelf of the best books, since if best for you or me, they may not be best for everybody.

A most learned man in India, in turning the leaves of a book, as he read, felt a little prick in his finger; a tiny snake dropped out and wriggled out of sight. The pundit's finger began to swell, then his arm; and in an hour, he was dead.

Who has not noticed in the home a snake in a book that has changed the character of a boy through its moral poison so that he was never quite the same again?

How well did Carlyle divide books into sheep and goats.

It is probable that the careers of the majority of criminals in our prisons to-day might have been vastly different if the character of their reading when they were young had been different; had it been uplifting, wholesome, instead of degrading.

"Christian Endeavor" Clark saw a notice conspicuously posted in a large city :~" All boys should read the wonderful story of the desperado brothers of the Western plains, whose strange and thrilling adventures of successful robbery and murder have never before been equaled. Price five cents." The next morning, Dr. Clark read in a newspaper of that city that seven boys had been arrested for burglary, and four stores broken into by the "gang." One of the ringleaders was only ten years old. At their trial, it appeared that each had invested five cents in the story of border crime. "Red-eyed Dick, the Terror of the Rockies," or some such story has poisoned many a lad's life. A seductive, demoralizing book destroys the ambition unless for vicious living. All that was sweet, beautiful, and wholesome in the character before seems to vanish, and everything changes after the reading of a single bad book. It has aroused the appetite for more forbidden pleasures, until it crowds out the desire for everything better, purer, healthier. Mental dissipation from this exciting literature, often dripping with suggestiveness of impurity, giving a passport to the prohibited, is fatal to all soundness of mind.

A lad once showed to another a book full of words and pictures of impurity. He only had it in his hands a few moments. Later in life he held high office in the church, and years afterward told a friend that he would have given half he possessed had he never seen that book.

Light, flashy stories, with no moral to them, seriously injured the mind of a brilliant young lady I once knew. Like the drug fiend whose brain has been stupefied, her brain became completely demoralized by constant mental dissipation. Familiarity with the bad ruins the taste for the good. Her ambition and ideas of life became completely changed. Her only enjoyment was the excitement of her imagination through vicious, unhealthful literature.

Nothing else will more quickly injure a good mind than familiarity with the frivolous, the superficial. Even though they may not be actually vicious, the reading of books which are not true to life, which carry home no great lesson, teach no sane or healthful philosophy, but are merely written to excite the passions, to stimulate a morbid curiosity, will ruin the best of minds in a very short time. It tends to destroy the ideals and to ruin the taste for all good reading.

In our reading we can take, in secret, the poison which kills, or we can drink in encouragement and inspiration which bids us look up. The poison in some books is extremely dangerous, because so subtle; the evil is often painted to look like good. Beware of books which, though they may not contain a single bad word, yet reek with immoral suggestions.

The spirit which pervades a book, the subtle motive in the author's mind when he wrote it, has everything to do with its influence. Read books which make you look up, which inspire you to be a little bigger man or woman, to amount to a little more in the world.

Read books that make you think more of yourself and believe more in yourself and in others. Beware of books that shake your confidence in your fellow-man. Read constructive books, books that are builders; avoid those that tear down. Beware of authors who sap your faith in men and your respect for womanhood, who shake your faith in the sanctity of the home and scoff at religion, who undermine sense of duty and moral obligation.

The books which we handle most often and value the highest are great tell-tales of our tastes and our ambition. A stranger could write a pretty good biography of a man he had never seen by careful examination and analysis of his reading matter.

Read, read, read all you can. But never read a bad book or a poor book. Life is too short, time too precious, to spend it in reading anything but the best.

Any book is bad for you, the reading of which takes away your desire for a better one.

Many people still hold that it is a bad thing for the young to read works of fiction. They believe that young minds get a moral twist from reading that which they know is not true, the descriptions of mere imaginary heroes and heroines, and of things which never happened. Now, this is a very narrow, limited view of a big question. These people do not understand the office of the imagination; they do not realize that many of the fictitious heroes and heroines that live in our minds, even from childhood's days, are much more real in their influence on our lives than some of those that exist in flesh and blood.

Dickens' marvelous characters seem more real to us than any we have ever met.' They have followed millions of people from childhood to old age, and influenced their whole lives for good. Many of us would look upon it as a great calamity to have these characters of fiction blotted out of our memory and their influence taken out of our lives.

Readers are sometimes so wrought up by a good work of fiction, their minds raised to such a pitch of courage and daring, their faculties so sharpened and braced, their whole nature so stimulated, that they can for the time being attempt and accomplish things which were impossible to them without the stimulus.

This, it seems to me, is one of the great values of fiction. If it is good and elevating, it is a splendid exercise of all the mental and moral faculties; it increases courage; it rouses enthusiasm; it sweeps the brain-ash off the mind, and actually strengthens its ability to grasp new principles and to grapple with the difficulties of life.

Many a discouraged soul has been refreshened, reinvigorated, has taken on new life by the reading of a good romance. I recall a bit of fiction, called "The Magic Story," which has helped thousands of discouraged souls, given them new hope, new life, when they were ready to give up the struggle.

The reading of good fiction is a splendid imagination exerciser and builder. It stimulates it by suggestions, powerfully increases its picturing capacity, and keeps it fresh and vigorous and wholesome, and a wholesome imagination plays a very great part in every . sane and worthy life. It makes it possible for us to shut out the most disagreeable past, to shut out at will all hideous memories of our mistakes, failures, and misfortunes; it helps us to forget our trouble and sorrows, and to slip at will into a new, fresh world of our own making, a world which we can make as beautiful, as sublime, as we wish. The imagination is a wonderful substitute for wealth, luxuries, and for material things. No matter how poor we may be, or how unfortunate-we may be bedridden even-we can by its aid travel round the world, visit its greatest cities, and create the most beautiful things for ourselves.

Sir John Herschel tells an amusing anecdote illustrating the pleasure derived from a book, not assuredly of the first order. In a certain village a blacksmith got hold of Richardson's novel "Pamela, or Virtue Rewarded," and used to sit on his anvil in the long summer evenings and read it aloud to a large and attentive audience. It is by no means a short book, but they fairly listened to it all. "At length, when the happy turn of fortune arrived, which brings the hero and heroine together and sets them living long and happily according to the most approved rules, the congregation were so delighted as to raise a great shout, and, procuring the church keys, actually set the parish bells ringing."

"It all comes back to us now," said the editor of the *Interior* not long ago, "that winter evening in the old home. The curtains are down, the fire is sending out a cheerful warmth and the shaded lamp diffusing a well-tempered radiance. The lad of fifteen is bent over a borrowed volume of sea tales. For hours he reads on, oblivious of all surroundings, until parental attention is drawn toward him by the unusual silence. The boy is seen to be trembling from head to foot with suppressed excitement. A fatherly hand is laid upon the volume, closing it firmly, and the edict is spoken, 'No more novels for five years.' And the lad goes off to bed, half glad, half grieved, wondering whether he has found fetters or achieved freedom.

"In truth he had received both; for that undiscriminating command forbade to him, during a formative period of his life, works which would have kindled his imagination, enriched his fancy, and heightened his power of expression; but it saved him from a possible descent to the Inferno; it made heroes of history, not demigods of mythology, his companions, and reserved to maturer years those excursions in the literature of the imagination which may lead a young man up to heaven or as easily drag him down to hell.

"There was never such a demand for fiction as now, and never larger opportunities for its usefulness. Nothing has such an attraction for life as life. But what the heart craves is not , life as it is.' It is life as it ought to be. We want not the feeble but the forceful; not the commonplace but the transcendent. Nobody objects to the 'purpose novel' except those who object to the purpose. Dealing as it does, in the hands of a great master, with the grandest passions, the most tender emotions, the divinest hopes, it can portray all these spiritual forces in their majestic sweep and uplift. And as a matter of history, we have seen the novel achieve in a single generation the task at which the homily had labored ineffectively for a hundred years. Realizing this, it is safe to say that there is not a theory of the philosopher, a hope of the reformer, or a prayer of the saint which does not eventually take form in a story. The novel has wings, while logic plods with a staff. In the hour it takes the metaphysician to define his premises, the story-teller has reached the goal and after him : tumbles the crowd tumultuous."

Arranged in the order of their popularity, as decided by the readers of the *Literary News* some years ago, the following are the world's ten best novels:

David Copperfield, Dickens. Ivanhoe, Eliot; The Letter Scarlet, Hawthorne; Uncle Tom's Cabin, Stow; The Newcomes, Thackeray; Les Miserables, Victor Hugo; John Halifax, Gentleman; Mulock, Craik.

The ten next best novels, as decided by the same constituency, and constituting, with the foregoing list of ten, the world's most popular twenty, are:

Kenilworth, Scott Henry Esmond; Thackeray, Romola; George Eliot, The Last Days of Pompeii; Lytton, Middlemarch; Eliot, The Marble; Faun, Hawthorne; Pendennis, Thackeray;Hypatia, Charles Kingsley; The House of Seven Gables, Hawthorne; The Mill on the Floss, George Eliot.

To those who enjoy novels with strong underlying themes, this list, prepared by Hamilton Wright Mabie for the *Ladies' Home Journal,* will offer a delightful range for selection:

" PROBLEM" NOVELS

Red Pottage by Cholmondeley; The Awakening of Helena Richie by Deland; Philip and His Wife by Deland; The Patriot; The Saint; The Sinner, all by Fogazzaro; The Undercurrent; and Unleavened Bread, both by Grant. Tess of the D'Urbervilles by Hardy; The Common Lot, and Her Son, by Herrick Vachell; The House of Mirth and The Fruit of the Tree by Wharton.

NOVELS ON SOCIOLOGICAL SUBJECTS

Put Yourself in His Place, & It Is Never Too Late to Mend, both by Reade; Felix Holt, the Radical by Eliot; All Sorts and Conditions of Men by Besant; The Pit by Norris; Fathers and Sons by Turgenief; Truth by Zola; Looking Backward by Bellamy; Beggars All by Dougall

NOVELS OF PLOT

The Moonstone by Collins; Treasure Island by Stevenson; Jane Eyre, Bronte; The Heart of Midlothian by Scott; Notre Dame de Paris, Victor Hugo; It Is Never Too Late to Mend & Reade The Mill on the Floss; Eliot Under the Greenwood Tree, all by Hardy; Our Mutual Friend by Dickens; The Three Musketeers by Dumas; Monte Cristo by Dumas

NOVELS OF CHARACTER STUDY

Pride and Prejudice, Austen; Sentimental Tommy, by Barrie; Middlemarch by Eliot; Anna Karenina, Tolstoi; Joseph Vance, De Morgan; The Mayor of Chesterbridge, Hardy; The Scarlet Letter, Hawthorne; The Rise of Silas & Lapham, by Howells;The Portrait of a Lady, James; The Egoist, Meredith; The Sanctuary, Wharton; Divine Fire, Sinclair; Vanity Fair by Thackeray; Dr. Jekyll and Mr. Hyde, Stevenson.

NOVELS OF REALISM

Anna Karenina by Tolstoi; Daisy Miller, and The Bostoriians, by James; Adam Bede by Eliot; The Mill on the Floss Eliot Oliver Twist Dickens A Pair of Blue Eyes , " . Hardy Hazard of New Fortunes Howells The House of Mirth Wharton The Common Lot Herrick

ROMANTIC NOVELS

Notre Dame de Paris, Victor Hugo; David Balfour; St Ives, & Prince Otto, all by Stevenson; To Have and to Hold by Johnston; Charles O'Malley by Lever; Guy Mannering by Scott; Quentin Durward Scott; Marble Faun by Hawthorne; Mr. Isaacs by Crawford

NOVELS OF HUMOR

The Vicar of Wakefield, Goldsmith; Deephaven by Hardy; Rudder Grange by Jewett; Oldtown Folks by Stockt; Don Quixote by Cervantes;

Sir John Lubbock, included in his list of "The Hundred Best Books the following representatives of Modern Fiction:

Either Emma *or* Pride and Prejudice by Austen; Vanity Fair and Pendennis by Thackeray; Pickwick *and* David Copperfield by Dickens; Adam Bede by George Eliot; Last Days of Pompeii by Bulwer; Lytton Scott's Novels

The graded list of books for young people which follows was compiled by Hamilton Wright Mabie. It will be appreciated especially by teachers and parents.

Books for Children Under Five Years of Age

GIRLS

Mother Goose, Classic Nursery Tales-Cinderella; The Three Bears; Little Red Riding Hood; Hop; My Thumb, etc. Fables and Folk Stories, H. E. Scudder, The Storyland, Elizabeth Harrison. In the Child's World, Emilie Poulsson. Small Songs for Small Singers, The Story Hour, Kate D. Wiggin and Nora A. Smith; The Good Fairy and the Bunnies, Allen A. Green; Cat Stories, Helen Hunt Jackson. Bible Stories '

BOYS

Mother Goose (Illustrated edition by Nister) The Book of the Zoo; The Book of the Farm; The Moo Cow Book; Our Dog Friends, Animal Books by Ernest Nister; Fables and Folk Stories H. E. Scudder Fairy Tales Grimm's and Andersen's The Stories Mother Nature Told Her Children, by Jane Andrews; Child's Garden of Verses by R. L. Stevenson. Aesop's Fables. Bible Stories

For Children from Five to Ten Years of Age

GIRLS

Alice in Wonderland and Through the Looking Glass, by Lewis Carroll; Lullaby-Land (Eugene Field); The Seven Little Sisters by Jane Andrews; Primer of Work and Play by Edith G. Alger; Little Goody Two Shoes (Edited by Charles Welsh); Miss Muffet's Christmas Party by Samuel M. Crothers; Goops and How to be Them; More Goops and How Not to be Them by Gelett Burgess; Hiawatha by Longfellow; Five Minute Stories by Laura E. Richards. Also The Little Lame Prince; The Adventures of a Brownie (Dinah Maria Mulock); Craik The Peterkin Papers (Lucretia Hale); Legends of King Arthur by Frances N. Greene; The Rose and the Ring by Thackeray; Child Stories from the Masters by Maud Menefee; At the Back of the North Wind by George Macdonald; Ballads for Little Folk by Alice and Phoebe Cary

BOYS

The King of the Golden River, Ruskin; Water Babies, Kingsley; Just So Stories, Kipling; Nights with Uncle Remus by Harris; Glimpses of Nature for Little Folks, K. A. Griel; Crib and Fly: A Tale of Two Terriers, (Edited by Charles Welsh); The Boy's King Arthur by Sidney Lanier; Wonder Book of Horses; Story of Roland; Story of Siegfried; Story of the Golden Age, all by James Baldwin; Visit to London by E. V. Lucas; Toby Tyler by James Otis; Gods and Heroes R. E. Francillon; Buz by Maurice Noel. The Jungle Book; The Second Jungle Book by Kipling; Rab and His Friends by Dr. John Brown; Black Beauty byAnna Sewell; Ten Boys Who Lived on the Road from Long Ago to Now by Jane Andrews; Stories of Great Americans by Edward Eggleston; Wonder Book and Tanglewood Tales, by Hawthorne

For Children from Ten to Fifteen Years of Age

GIRLS

Little Women; Little Men; An Old-Fashioned Girl; Under the Lilacs; Jo's Boys, all by Louisa M. Alcott

Two Little Waifs; Us Mrs. Molesworth Tales from Shakespeare Lamb Franconia Stories Jacob Abbott Sara Crewe; Little St. Elizabeth

Mrs. Burnett Pilgrim's Progress Bunyan Silas Marner; The Mill on the Floss, all by George Eliot

Undine, Foque; Lorna Doone by Blackmore; Hildegard Series (5) Laura E. Richards The Little Minister J. M. Barrie Rebecca of Sunnybrook Farm, Kate D. Wiggin Rebecca of Sunnybrook Farm; New Chronicles of Rebecca by Kate D. Wiggin; Adventures of Dorothy by Jocelyn Lewis; Gypsy Books by Elizabeth Stuart Phelps Ward; Little Pussy by Willow; Harriet Beecher by Stowe; Six to Sixteen by Juliana Horatia Ewing; Memories of a London Doll,

Mrs. Fairstar; Toinette's Philip by C. V. Jamison; Abbe Constantin by Ludovic Halevy; The Daisy Chain and Pillars of the House by Charlotte M. Yonge

BOYS

Arabian Nights, Large edition

J. Fenimore Cooper's Novels

Jolly Fellowship, Stockton

The Nurnberg Stove, Ouida

The Hoosier School-Boy, Edward Eggleston

The Land of the Midnight Sun,. Du Chaillu

Tom Brown's School Days by Hughes

Two Years Before the Mast, R H. Dana

Two Little Savages by E. Thompson Seton

Boy's Life of Lincoln .by Helen Nicolay

The Hill H. A. Vachell

Stories of Adventure; Boys' Heroes, E. E. Hale

Squirrels and Other Fur-Bearers; Birds and Bees by Burroughs.

Treasure Island by Stevenson

The Story of a Bad Boy by Aldrich.

Masterman Ready F. Marryat

The Swiss Family Robinson by J. R Wyss

Rip Van Winkle; The Legend of Sleepy Hollow by Irving

Around the World in the Sloop Spray" J. Slocum.

Boys of Other Countries, Bayard Taylor.

Two Little Confederates, Thomas Nelson Page

Aztec Treasure House, Thomas A. Janvier

Westward Ho, by Kingsley

Birds Through an Opera Glass, F. A. Merriam Bailey

Translation of the Odyssey ..... G. H. Palmer

Three Greek Children; Story of the Iliad, Young

Knocking 'Round the Rockies, by Ernest Ingersoll.

Hans Brinker, by Mary Mapes Dodge

The Half Back; Behind the Line by Ralph Henry Barbour

Life of Garfield W. O. Stoddard The Man Without a Country E. E. Hale Blue Jackets of 1898; Battle Fields of '61, W. J. Abbot

Plutarch for Boys and Girls .. " John S. White

Heart, a School-boy's Journal (trans. by Isabel Hapgood) by Edmondo De Amicis

Days of Ancient Rome by Macaulay

Harold, by Lytton

For Young People from Fifteen to Twenty
Years of Age

''' GIRLS

John Halifax, Gentleman .. Mrs. Mulock-Craik, New England Nun and Other Stories, by Mary E. Wilkins

T. B. Aldrich's Short Stories

Jane Austen's Novels

Charles Reade's Novels

Essays of Elia, by Lamb

Sesame and Lilies; Crown of Wild Olive

Ruskin

Little Rivers; The Ruling Passion, by Henry van Dyke

Uarda; Homo Sum; .Ebers Gold by Elsie E. Marlitt

To Have and to Hold by Mary Johnston

Thomas Nelson Page's Short Stories

Santilario : Saracinesca; Corleone; MariettaF. Marion Crawford Penelope in England; Penelope's Progress; Penelope in Ireland .•

Kate Douglas Wiggin The Rise of Silas Lapham; An Indian Summer
. Howells Little Masterpieces of English Poetry by British and
American Authors Henry van Dyke and Hardin Craig

American Anthology; Victorian Anthology by Stedman

BOYS

Ben Hur by Lew Wallace; Rob Roy; Ivanhoe; The Heart of
Midlothian; The Abbot; Kenilworth; The Pirate; Boys' and Girls'
Plutarch, all by Sir Walter Scott; The Sketch-Book by Washington
Irving; The Autocrat of the Breakfast Table, Holmes.
Representative Men, by Emerson. Fenimore Cooper's Novels. Kim;
Captain Courageous, Kipling. Jack Hazard, J. T. Trowbridge.
Kidnaped; David Balfour; The Master of Ballantrae by Stevenson.
Henry Esmond; The Virginians; The Newcomes; Pendennis, all by
Thackeray

David Copperfield; Nicholas Nickleby; Martin Chuzzlewit; Tale
of Two Cities, by Dickens. Francis Parkman's Histories.
Biographies in the Great Writers Series Biographies in the
American Statesmen Series Biographies in the American Men of
Letters

Series

Three Guardsmen; The Black Tulip .... Dumas

The Call of the Wild Jack London

The Cloister and the Hearth; Put Yourself in His Place Charles
Reade The Man with the Broken Ear; The King of the Mountains
Edmond About The Virginian Owen Wister

Short Stories of the English People, J.R Green

John Fiske's Histories

The Rise of the Dutch Republic by J. L. Motley; Brave Little
Holland by W. E. Griffin; Ferdinand and Isabella by Prescott
Charles the Fifth; William Robertson The American Revolution by
G. O. Trevelyan; Charles the Bold J. F. Kirk; Makers of Florence;
Makers of Venice; Royal Edinburgh, all by Mrs. Oliphant; Ave

Roma Immortalis F. Marion Crawford The Story of Germany S. B. Gould The Story of Norway by H. H. Boyesen The Conquest of Mexico by Prescott; Heroes of the Middle West, Mrs. Catherwood; The Conquest by Dye; Beginnings of a Nation by Edward Eggleston; Americans of 1776 by Schouler; The Winning of the West by Roosevelt; Life of Cesar, Froude; Life of Johnson, Boswell; Early Life of Charles James, Fox; Life of Macaulay by Trevelyan; Life of Scott by Lockhart; Life of Nelson by Southey; The Four Georges by Thackeray; Life of Lincoln by Nicolay and Hay; Life of Robert E. Lee by John Esten Cook or W. P. Trent; George Washington by Horace E. Scudder; Holmes, Oliver Cromwell, by John Morley; Ralph Waldo Emerson.

11

READING, A SPUR TO AMBITION

> I know of nothing else which will enlarge one's ideals and lift one's life standards more than the study of the lives of great and noble characters; the reading of biographies of great men and women. Abroad, it is impossible for me to avoid the society of fools. In my study, I can call up the ablest spirits, the learnedest philosophers, the wisest counselors, the greatest generals, and make them serviceable to me.-SIR WILLIAM WALLER.

THE great purpose in reading is for self-discovery. Inspirational, character-making, life-shaping books are helpful to this end.

There are books that have raised the ideals and materially influenced entire nations. Who can estimate the value of books that spur ambition, that awaken slumbering possibilities?

Cotton Mather's it Essay to Do Good" influenced the whole career of Benjamin Franklin, we are told.

Are we ambitious to associate with people who inspire us to nobler deeds? Let us then read uplifting books, which stir us to make the most of ourselves.

We all know how completely changed we sometimes are after reading a book which has taken a strong, vigorous hold upon us.

Thousands of people have found themselves through the reading of some book which has opened the door within them and given them the first glimpse of their possibilities. I know men and women whose whole lives have been molded, the entire trend of their careers completely changed, uplifted beyond their fondest dreams, by the good books they have taken time to read.

It has been said by President White of Cornell that, "The great thing needed to be taught in this country is *truth, simple ethics, the distinction between right and wrong.* Stress should be laid upon *what is best in biography,* upon *noble deeds and sacrifices,* especially those which show that the greatest man is not the greatest orator, or the tricky politician. They are a curse; what we need is *noble men.* National loss comes as the penalty for frivolous boyhood and girlhood, that gains no moral stamina from wholesome books."

If youths learn to feed on the thoughts of the great men and women of all times, they will never again be satisfied with the common or low; they will never again be content with mediocrity; they will aspire to some thing higher and nobler.

A day which is passed without treasuring up some good thought is not well spent. Every day is a leaf in the book of life.

The Bible, such manuals as " Daily Strength for Daily Needs," such books as Professor C. C. Everett's "Ethics for Young People"; Lucy Elliot Keeler's" IfI Were a Girl Again";

"Beauty through Hygiene," by Dr. Emma F. Walker; such essays as Robert L. Stevenson's

"Gentlemen" (in his "Familiar Studies of Men and Books "); Smiles' "Self Help"; John Ruskin's" Sesame and Lilies"; and, according to a statement made a few years ago by Hamilton Wright Mabie in the *Ladies' Home Journal,* the author's Inspirational Book, "Pushing to the Front "-this is literature that makes young men and women trustworthy, so that the Marshall Fields and John Wanamakers want their aid in the conduct of great business concerns. Blessed are they who go much farther in later years, and who become familiar with those

"Olympian bards who sang

Divine ideas below,

Which always find us young

And always keep us so."

The readers who do not know the Concord philosopher Emerson, and the great writers of antiquity, Marcus Aurelius, Epictetus, and Plato, have pleasures to come.

Aside from reading fiction, books of travel are of the best for mental diversion; then there are nature studies, and science and poetry, all affording wholesome recreation, all of an uplifting character, and some of them opening up study specialties of the highest order, as in the great range of books classified as Natural Science.

The reading and study of poetry is much like the interest one takes in the beauties of natural scenery. Much of the best poetry is indeed a poetic interpretation of nature. Whittier and Longfellow and Bryant lead their readers to look on nature with new eyes, as Ruskin opened the eyes of Henry Ward Beecher.

A great deal of the best prose is in style and sentiment of a true poetic character, lacking only the metrical form. To become familiar with Tennyson and Shakespeare and the brilliant catalogue of British poets is in itself a liberal education. Rolfe's Shakespeare is in handy volumes, and so edited as to be of most service. Palgrave's" Golden Treasury," of the best songs and lyrical poems in the English language, was edited with the advice and collaboration of Tennyson. His" Children's Treasury" of lyrical poetry is most attractive. Emerson's" Parnassus," and Whittier's" Three Centuries of Song" are excellent collections of the most famous poems of the ages.

Never before was a practical substitute for a college education at home made so cheap, so easy, and so desirable. Knowledge of all kinds is placed before us in an attractive and interesting manner. The best of the literature of the world is found to-day in thousands of American homes where fifty years ago it could only have been obtained by the rich.

What a shame it is that under such conditions as these an American should grow up ignorant, should be uneducated in the midst of such marvelous opportunities for self-improvement! Indeed, most of the best literature in every line to-day appears in the current periodicals, in the form of short articles. Many of our greatest writers spend a vast amount of time in the drudgery of travel and investigation, in gathering material for these articles, and the magazine publishers pay thou- sands of dollars for what a reader can get for ten or fifteen cents. Thus the reader secures for a trifle in periodicals or books the results of months and often years of hard work and investigation of our greatest writers.

A New York millionaire, a prince among merchants, took me over his palatial residence on Fifth A venue, every room of which was a triumph of the architect's, of the decorator's, and of the upholsterer's art. I was told that the decorations of a single sleeping room had cost ten thousand dollars. On the walls were paintings which cost fabulous prices, and about the rooms were pieces of massive and costly furniture and draperies representing a small fortune, and covering the floors were carpets on which it seemed almost sacrilege to tread. He had expended a fortune for physical pleasure, comfort, luxury, and display, but there was scarcely a book in the house. It was pitiful to think of the physical surfeit and mental starvation of the children of such a home as that. He told me that he came to the city a poor boy, with all his worldly possessions done up in a little red bandanna. "I am a millionaire," he said, "but

I want to tell you that I would give half

I have to-day for a decent education."

Many a rich man has confessed to confidential friends and his own heart that he would give much of his wealth, all, if necessary, to see his son a manly man, free from the habits which abundance has formed and fostered till they have culminated in sin and degradation and perhaps crime; and has realized that, in all his ample provision, he has failed to provide that which might have saved his son and himself from loss and torture, good books in the home.

There is a wealth within the reach of the poorest mechanic and day-laborer in this country that kings in olden times could not possess, and that is the wealth of a well-read, cultured mind. In this newspaper age, this age of cheap books and periodicals, there is no excuse for ignorance, for a coarse, untrained mind. To-day no one is so handicapped, if he have health and the use of his faculties, that he cannot possess himself of wealth that will enrich his whole life, and enable him to converse and mingle with the most cultured people. No one is so poor but that it is possible for him to lay hold of that which will broaden his mind, which will inform and improve him, and lift him out of the brute stage of existence into the godlike realm of knowledge.

"No entertainment is so cheap as reading," says Mary Wortley Montague; "nor any pleasure so lasting." Good books elevate the character, purify the taste, *take the attractiveness out of low pleasures,* and lift us upon a higher plane of thinking and living.

"A great part of what the British spend on books," says Sir John Lubbock, " they save in prisons and police."

It seems like a miracle that the poorest boy can converse freely with the greatest philosophers and scientists, statesmen, warriors, authors of all time, with little expense, that the inmates of the humblest cabin may follow the stories of the nations, the epochs of history, the story of liberty, the romance of the world, and the course of human progress.

Carlyle said that a collection of books is a university. What a pity that the thousands of ambitious, energetic men and women who missed their opportunities for an education at the school age, and feel crippled by their loss, fail to catch the-significance of this, fail to realize the tremendous cumulative possibilities of that great life-improver, that admirable substitute for a college or university education -reading.

Have you just been to a well-educated, sharp-sighted employer to find work? You did not need to be at any trouble to tell him the names of the books you have read, because they have left their indelible mark upon your face and your speech. Your pinched, starved vocabulary, your lack of polish, your slang expressions, tell him of the trash to which you have given your precious time. He knows that you have not rightly systemized your hours. He knows that thousands of young men and women whose lives are crowded to overflowing with routine work and duties, manage to find time to keep posted on what is going on in the world, and for systematic, useful reading.

"Of the things which man can do or make here below," it was said by the Sage of Chelsea, "by far the most momentous, wonderful, and worthy are the things we call books! Those poor bits of rag-paper with black ink on them; from the daily newspaper to the sacred Hebrew Book, what have they not done, what are they not doing?"

President Schurmann of Cornell points with pride to a few books in his library which he says he bought when a poor boy by going many a day without his dinner.

The great German Professor Oken was not ashamed to ask Professor Agassiz to dine with him on potatoes and salt, that he might save money for books.

King George III. used to say that lawyers do not know so much more law than people of other callings, but that they know better where to find it.

A practical working knowledge of how to find what is in the book world, relating to any given point, is worth a vast deal from a financial point of view. And by such knowledge, one forms first an acquaintance with books, then friendship.

"When I consider," says James Freeman Clarke, "what some books have done for the world, and what they are doing, how they keep up our hope, awaken new courage and faith, soothe pain, give an ideal of life to those whose homes are hard and cold, bind together distant ages and foreign lands, create new worlds of beauty, bring down truths from heaven, I give eternal blessings for this gift."

Not long ago President Eliot of Harvard College aroused widespread controversy over his selection of a library of books which might be contained on a five-foot shelf, in the belief that "the faithful and considerate reading of these books will give any man a liberal education even if he can devote to them but fifteen minutes a day." The titles of the books so far selected are:

The Autobiography of Benjamin Franklin

The Journal of John Woolman

Some Fruits of Solitude William Penn

The Apology, Phredo, and Crito (translated by Benjamin Jowett) Plato The Golden Sayings of Epictetus (translated by H. Crossley)

The Meditations of Marcus Aurelius (translated by J. S. Long)

The Essays of Francis Bacon

The New Atlantis (Spedding Text), Francis Bacon

Areopagitica; Tractate on Education (John Milton)

The Complete Poems of John Milton

Religio Medici,Sir Thomas Browne Essays and English Traits, Ralph Waldo Emerson

The Poems of Robert Burns

The Confessions of St. Augustine (Pusey Text) The Imitation of Christ .... Thomas a Kernpis

Nine Greek Dramas; Agamemnon, The Libation-Bearers, The Furies (translated by E. D. A. Morshead);

Aeschylus Prometheus, Aeschylus

Oedipus the King, Antigone by Sophocles

Hippolytus, The Bacchze (translated by Gilbert Murray)

Euripides, The Frogs, Aristophanes

The Letters of Cicero (translated by E. S. Shuckburgh)

Cicero's Treatise on Friendship and Old Age (translated by W. Melmoth)

The Letters of Pliny (revised by F. C. T. Bosanquet)

The Wealth of Nations (edited by Professor J.C. Bullock, Harvard University) Adam Smith

The Origin of Species by Charles Darwin

Lives of Themistocles, Pericles, Aristides, Alcibiades, Coriolanus, Demosthenes, Cicero, Caesar, Antony (from the translation known as Dryden's corrected and revised by Arthur Hugh Clough); Plutarch The Aeneid (translated by John Dryden), Virgil

Don Quixote, Cervantes

Pilgrim's Progress John Bunyan

The Lives of Donne and Herbert

Izaak Walton

Stories from the Arabian Nights (Stanley

Lane-Poole translation) Folk-Lore and Fables: Aesop's Fables, 82 titles.

Grimm's Household Tales, 41 titles

Tales from Hans Christian Andersen, 20 titles

Modern English Drama:

All for Love, John Dryden

The School for Scandal

Richard Brinsley, Sheridan

She Stoops to Conquer Oliver Goldsmith

The Cenci, Percy Bysshe Shelley

A Blot in the Scutcheon, Robert Browning

Manfred Lord Byron

Faust, Hermann and Dorothea, Egrnont Goethe

Doctor Faustus Christopher Marlowe

The Divine Comedy, Dante

I Promessi Sposi, Alessandro Manzoni

The Odyssey of Homer (Butcher and Lang translation)

Two Years Before the Mast, Richard Henry Dana, Jr.

Essays on Taste; on the Sublime and Beautiful; Reflections on the French Revolution; Letter to a Noble Lord Edmund Burke

Essays on Liberty; Autobiography, John Stuart Mill

Inaugural Address as Lord Rector of Edinburgh University; Characteristics; Essay on Scott .by Thomas Carlyle

Continental Drama:

Calderon

Corneille

Lessing

Moliere

Racine

English Essays:

Abraham Cowley John Locke Jonathan Swift Samuel Johnson Sydney Smith William Hazlitt Coleridge

Leigh Hunt

Charles Lamb Thomas de Quincey Joseph Addison

Sir Richard Steele

Daniel Defoe

David Hume

Percy Bysshe Shelley

Thomas B. Macaulay

English and American Essays:

Cardinal Newman Dean Swift

John Ruskin Matthew Arnold James A. Froude Walter Bagehot Edward A. Freeman Thomas H. Huxley

Edgar Allan Poe Robert Louis Stevenson

James Russell Lowell Henry D. Thoreau

William Makepeace Thackeray

The Voyage of the Beagle .... Charles Darwin

Scientific Papers-Chemistry, Physics, Astronomy:

Faraday

Lord Kelvin

Helmholtz

Newcomb

Essays-French, German, Italian:

Montaigne Renan Schiller Grimm Kant

Mazzini Sainte-Beuve Lessing Goethe

Ancient and Elizabethan Voyages and Travels:

Herodotus

Sir Francis Drake

Sir Humphrey Gilbert

Coronado

Descartes, Voltaire, etc.

Tacitus

Sir Walter Raleigh

Magellan

Captain John Smith

Scientific Papers-Biology, Medicine, etc., including articles by Sir John Lister and Ambroise Pare

Famous Prefaces

Caxton

Raleigh

John Knox

Heminge and Condell

Fielding

Schiller Whitman Berners

Spenser Calvin Bacon Dryden Johnson Taine Wordsworth Newton

American Historical Documents, containing 40 important documents, such as:

Cabots' Voyage

Columbus's Letter

First Charter of Virginia

Mayflower Compact

Cornwallis's Proposal of Surrender

Washington's First Inaugural

Monroe Doctrine

Lincoln's First Inaugural

Lincoln's Second Inaugural

Chronicles

National Epics

Machiavelli, More, and others Comparative Religions and Hymns; Elizabethan Dramas.

Ex-President Theodore Roosevelt selected for his famous African trip the following books:

Bible

Apocrypha

Bible in Spain; Zingali; Lavengro; Wild Wales; The Romany Rye, all by Borrow

Shakespeare

Faerie Queene by Spenser

Marlowe

Sea Power, Mahan

History; Essays; Poems, Macaulay

Iliad; Odyssey, Homer

La Chanson de Roland

Nibelungen Lied

Frederick the Great, Carlyle

Poems, Shelley

Essays by Bacon

Literary Essays; Biglow Papers

Lowell Poems

Emerson

Longfellow

Tennyson

Tales; Poems by Poe

Keats

Paradise Lost (Books I. & II) Milton; Inferno (Carlyle's translation) Dante; Autocrat; Over the Teacups; Holmes Poems; Tales of the Argonauts; Luck of Roaring Camp Bret Harte Selections by Browning; Gentle Reader by Crothers; Huckleberry Finn and Tom Sawyer by Mark Twain; Pilgrim's Progress by Bunyan; Hippolytus; Bacchre (Murray's translation); Euripides; The Federalist; Rome by GregoroviusM Legend of Montrose; Guy Mannering; Waverley; Rob Roy, .Antiquary by Scott Pilot; Two Admirals by Cooper; Froissart; Percy's Reliques; Vanity Fair; Pendennis byThackeray; Mutual Friend; Pickwick, by Dickens

Colonel Roosevelt says: "The list represents in part Kermit's taste, in part mine; and, I need hardly say, it also represents in no way all the books we most care for, but merely those which, for one reason or another, we thought we should like to take on this particular trip."

It is the author's hope and desire that the lists given, limited as they are, may prove of value to those seeking self-education, and that the books may encourage the disheartened, stimulate ambition, and serve as steppingstones to higher ideals and nobler purposes in life.

12

THE SELF-IMPROVEMENT HABIT, A GREAT ASSET

A boy is better unborn than untaught. GASCOIGNE.

It is ignorance that wastes; it is knowledge that saves, an untaught faculty is at once quiescent and dead.-N. D. HILLIS.

The plea that this or that man has no time for culture will vanish as soon as we desire culture so much that we begin to examine seriously into our present use of time.-MATTHEW ARNOLD.

EDUCATION, as commonly understood, is the process of developing the mind by means of books and teachers. When education has been neglected, either by reason of lack of opportunity, or because advantage was not taken of the opportunities afforded, the one remaining hope is self-improvement. Opportunities for self-improvement surround us, the helps to self-improvement are abundant, and in this day of cheap books, free libraries, and evening schools, there can be no good excuse for neglect to use the faculties for mental growth and development which are so abundantly supplied.

When we look at the difficulties which hindered the acquisition of knowledge fifty years to a century ago; the scarcity and the costliness of books, the value of the dimmest candlelight, the unremitting toil which left so little time for study, the physical weariness which had to be overcome to enable mental exertion in study, we may well marvel at the giants of scholarship those days of hardship produced. And when we add to these limitations physical disabilities, blindness, deformity, ill-health, which many contended against, we may feel shame as we contemplate the fullness of modern opportunity and the helps and incentives to study and self-development which are so lavishly provided for our use and inspiration, and of which we avail ourselves so little.

Self-improvement implies one essential feeling: the desire for improvement. If the desire exists, then improvement is usually accomplished only by the conquest of self the material self, which seeks pleasure and amusement. The novel, the game of cards, the billiard cue, idle whittling and story-telling, will have to be eschewed, and every available moment of leisure turned to account. For all who seek self-improvement "there is a lion in the way," the lion of self-indulgence, and it is only by the conquest of this enemy that progress is assured.

Show me how a youth spends his evenings, his odd bits of time, and I will forecast his future. Does he look upon this leisure as precious, rich in possibilities, as containing golden material for his future life structure? Or does he look upon it as an opportunity for self-indulgence, for a light, flippant "good time"?

The way he spends his leisure will give the keynote of his life, will tell whether he is dead in earnest, or whether he looks upon life as a joke.

He may not be conscious of the terrible effect, the gradual deterioration of character which comes from a frivolous wasting of his evenings and half-holidays, but the character is being undermined just the same.

Young men are often surprised to find them selves dropping behind their competitors, but if they will examine themselves, they will find that they have stopped growing because they have ceased their effort to keep abreast of the times, to be widely read, to enrich their life with self-culture.

The right use of spare moments in reading and study is an indication of superior qualities. And in many historic cases the "spare" moments utilized for study were not spare in the sense of being the spare time of leisure. They were rather *spared* moments, moments spared from sleep, from meal times, from recreation.

Where is the boy to-day who has less chance to rise in the world than Elihu Burritt, apprenticed at sixteen to a blacksmith, in whose shop he had to work at the forge all the daylight, and often by candle-light? Yet he managed, by studying with a book before him at his meals, carrying it in his pocket that he might utilize every spare moment, and studying at night and on holidays, to pick up an excellent education in the odds and ends of time which most boys throwaway. While the rich boy and the idler were yawning and stretching and getting their eyes open, young Burritt had seized the opportunity and improved it.

He had a thirst for knowledge and a desire for self-improvement, which overcame every obstacle in his pathway. A wealthy gentleman offered to pay his expenses at Harvard, but Elihu said he could get his education him- self, even though he had to work twelve or fourteen hours a day at the forge. Here was a determined boy. He snatched every spare moment at the anvil and forge as if it were gold. He believed, with Gladstone, that thrift of time would repay him in after years with usury, and that waste of it would make him dwindle. Think of a boy working nearly all the daylight in a blacksmith shop, and yet finding time to study seven languages in a single year!

It is not lack of ability that holds men down but lack of industry. In many cases the employee has a better brain, a better mental capacity than his employer. But he does not improve his faculties. He dulls his mind by vicious habits. He spends his time and money at the pool table and in the saloon and as he grows old, and the harness of perpetual service galls him, he grumbles at his lack of luck, his limited opportunity.

The number of perpetual clerks is constantly being recruited by those who did not think it worthwhile as boys to learn to write a good hand or to master the fundamental branches of knowledge requisite in a business career. The ignorance common among young men and young women in factories, stores, and offices, everywhere, in fact, in this land of opportunity where youth should be well educated, is a pitiable thing. On every hand we see men and women of natural ability occupying inferior positions because they did not think it of enough importance in their youth to concentrate their attention on the acquisition of knowledge that would make them proficient workers.

Thousands of men and women find them selves held back, handicapped for life, because of the seeming trifles which they did not think it worthwhile to pay attention to in their youth.

Many a girl of good natural ability spends her most productive years as a cheap clerk or in a mediocre position because she never thought it worthwhile to develop her mental faculties or to take advantage of opportunities within reach to fit herself for a superior position. Thousands of girls unexpectedly thrown on their own resources have been held down all their lives because of neglected tasks in youth, which at the time were dismissed with a careless" I don't think it worthwhile." They did not think it would pay to go to the bottom of any study at school, to learn to keep accounts accurately, or fit themselves to do anything in such a way as to be able to make a living by it. They expected to marry, and never prepared for being dependent on themselves, a contingency against which marriage, in many instances, is no safeguard.

The trouble with most youths is that they are not willing to fling the whole weight of their being into their vocation. They want short hours, little work and a lot of play. They think more of leisure and pleasure than of discipline and training in their great life specialty.

Many a clerk envies his employer and wishes that he could go into business for himself and be an employer also, but he thinks it is too much work to make the effort to rise above a clerkship. He likes to take life easy; and he wonders idly whether, after all, it is worthwhile to strain and strive and struggle and study to prepare oneself for the sake of getting up a little higher and making a little more money.

The trouble with a great many people is that they are not willing to make present sacrifices for future gain. They prefer to have a good time as they go along, rather than spend time in self-improvement. They have a vague wish to do something great, but few have that intensity of longing which impels them to make the sacrifice of the present for the future. Few are willing to work underground for years laying a foundation for their life structure. They yearn for greatness, but their yearning is not the kind which is willing to pay any price or make any sacrifice for its object.

So the majority slide along in mediocrity all their lives. They have ability for something higher up, but they have not the energy and determination to prepare for it. They do not care to make the necessary

·effort. They prefer to take life easier and lower down rather than to struggle for something higher. They do not play the game for all they are worth.

If a man or woman has but the disposition for self-improvement and advancement he will find opportunity to rise, or "what he cannot find, create." Here is an example from the everyday life going on around us and in which we are all taking part.

A young Irishman who had reached the age of nineteen or twenty without learning to read or write, and who left home because of the intemperance that prevailed there, learned to read a little by studying billboards, and eventually got a position as steward aboard a man of-war. He chose that occupation and got leave to serve at the captain's table because of a great desire to learn. He kept a little tablet in his coat-pocket, and whenever he heard a new word wrote it down. One day an officer saw him writing and immediately suspected him of being a spy. When he and the other officers learned what the tablet was used for, the young man was given more opportunities to learn, and these led in time to promotion, until, finally, he won a prominent position in the navy. Success as a naval officer prepared the way for success in other fields.

Self-help has accomplished about all the great things of the world. How many young men falter, faint, and dally with their purpose, because they have no capital to start with, and wait and wait for some good luck to give them a lift! But success is the child of hard work and perseverance. It cannot be coaxed or bribed; pay the price and it is yours.

One of the sad things about the neglected opportunities for self-improvement is that they put people of great natural ability at a disadvantage among those who are their mental inferiors.

I know a member of one of our state legislatures, a splendid fellow, immensely popular, who has a great, generous heart and broad sympathies, but who cannot open his mouth without so murdering the English language that it is really painful to listen to him.

There are a great many similar examples in Washington of men who have been elected to important positions because of their great natural ability and fine characters, but who are constantly mortified and embarrassed by their ignorance and lack of early training.

One of the most humiliating experiences that can ever come to a human being is to be conscious of possessing more than ordinary ability, and yet be tied to an inferior position because of lack of early and intelligent training commensurate with this ability. To know that one has ability to realize eighty or ninety per cent of his possibilities, but because of the lack of proper education and training, to be unable to bring out more than twenty-five per cent of it, is humiliating. In other words, to go through life conscious that you are making a botch of your capabilities just because of lack of training, is a most depressing, mortifying thing.

Nothing else outside of sin causes more sorrow than that which comes from not having prepared for the highest career possible to one. There are no more bitter regrets than those which result from being obliged to let pass opportunities for which one never prepared himself.

I know a pitiable case of a born naturalist whose ambition was so suppressed and whose education so neglected in youth that later, when he came to know more about natural history than almost any man of his day, he could not write a grammatical sentence, and could never make his ideas live in words, perpetuate them in books, because of his ignorance of even the rudiments of an education. His early vocabulary was so narrow and pinched, and his knowledge of his language so limited, that he always seemed to be painfully struggling for words to express his thought.

Think of the suffering of this splendid man, who was conscious of possessing colossal scientific knowledge, and yet was absolutely unable to express himself grammatically!

How often stenographers are mortified by the use of some unfamiliar word or term, or quotation, because of the shallowness of their preparation! It is not enough to be able to take dictation when ordinary letters are given, not enough to do the ordinary routine of office work. The ambitious stenographer must be prepared for the unusual word or expression, must have good reserves of knowledge to draw from in case of emergency. If she is constantly slipping up on her grammar, or is all at sea the moment she steps out of her ordinary routine, her employer knows that her preparation is shallow, that her education is limited, and her prospects will be limited also.

A young lady writes me that she is so handicapped by the lack of an early education that she fairly dreads to write a letter to anyone of education or culture for fear of making ignorant mistakes in grammar and spelling. Her letter indicates that she has considerable natural ability. Yet she is always placed at a disadvantage because of this lack of an early education. It is difficult to conceive of a greater misfortune than always to be embarrassed and handicapped just because of the neglect of early years.

I am often pained by letters from people, especially young people, which indicate that the writers have a great deal of natural ability, that they have splendid minds, but that a large part of their ability is covered up, rendered ineffectual by their lack of education.

Many of these letters show that the writers are like diamonds in the rough, with only here and there a little facet ground off, just enough to let in the light and reveal the great hidden wealth within.

I always feel sorry for such people who have passed the school age and who will probably go through life with their splendid minds handicapped by ignorance which, even late in life, they might largely or entirely overcome.

It is such a pity that a young man, for instance, who has the natural ability which would make him a leader among men, must, for the lack of a little training and preparation, work for somebody else, perhaps with scarcely half of his ability but with a better preparation, more education.

Everywhere we see clerks, mechanics, employees in all walks of life, who cannot rise to anything like positions which correspond with their natural ability, because they have not had the education. They are ignorant. They cannot write an intelligent letter. They murder the English language, and hence their superb ability cannot be demonstrated, and remains in mediocrity.

The parable of the talents illustrates and enforces one of nature's sternest laws: "To him that hath shall be given; from him that hath not shall be taken away even that which he hath." Scientists call this law the survival of the fittest. The fittest are those who use what they have, who gain strength by struggle, and who survive by self-development through control of their hostile or helpful environment.

The soil, the sunshine, the atmosphere are very liberal with the material for the growth of the plant or the tree, but the plant must use all it gets, must work it up into flowers, into fruit, into leaf or fiber or something, or the supply will cease. In other words, the soil will not send any more building material up the sap than is used for growth, and the

128

faster this material is used the more rapid the growth, the more abundantly the material will come.

The same law holds good everywhere. Nature is liberal with us if we utilize what she gives us, but if we stop using it, if we do not do some building somewhere, if we do not transform the material which she gives us into force and utilize that force, we not only find the supply cut off, but also that we are growing weaker, less efficient.

Everything in nature is on the move, either one way or the other. It is either going up or down. It is either advancing or retrograding; we cannot hold without using.

Nature withdraws muscle or brain if we do not use them. She withdraws skill the moment we stop using it efficiently. The force is withdrawn when we cease exercising it.

A college graduate is often surprised .years after he leaves his college to find that about all he has to show for his education is his diploma. The power and efficiency which he gained there have been lost because he has not been using them. He thought at the time when everything was still fresh in his mind, after his examination, that this knowledge would remain with him, but it has been slipping away from him every minute since he stopped using it, and only that has remained and increased which he has used; the rest has evaporated.

A great many college men ten years after graduation find that they have but very little to show for their four years' course, because they have not utilized their knowledge. They have become weaklings without knowing it. They constantly say to themselves, " I have a college education, I must have some ability, I must amount to something in the world." But the college diploma has no more power to hold the knowledge you have gained in college than a piece of tissue paper over a gas jet can hold the gas in the pipe.

Everything which you do not use is constantly slipping away from you. Use it or lose it. The secret of power is use. Ability will not remain with us; force will evaporate the moment we cease to do something with it.

The tools for self-improvement are at your hand. Use them. If the ax is dull the more strength must be put forth. If your opportunities are limited you must use more energy, put forth more effort. Progress may seem slow at first, but perseverance assures success. "Line upon line, and precept upon precept" is the rule of mental upbuilding, and" In due time ye shall reap if ye faint not."

13
THE RAISING OF VALUES

"Destiny is not about thee, but within, Thyself must make thyself."

THE world is no longer clay, but rather iron in the hands of its workers," says Emerson, "and men have got to hammer out a place for themselves by steady and rugged blows."

To make the most of your "stuff," be it cloth, iron, or character -this is success.

Raising common" stuff" to priceless value is great success.

The man who first takes the rough bar of wrought iron may be a blacksmith, who has only partly learned his trade, and has no ambition to rise above his anvil. He thinks that the best possible thing he can do with his bar is to make it into horseshoes, and congratulates himself upon his success. He reasons that the rough lump of iron is worth only two or three cents a pound, and that it is not worthwhile to spend much time or labor on it. His enormous muscles and small skill have raised the value of the iron from one dollar, perhaps, to ten dollars.

Along comes a cutler, with a little better education, a little more ambition, a little finer perception, and says to the blacksmith: "Is this all you can see in that iron? Give me a bar, and I will show you what brains and skill and hard work can make of it." He sees a little further into the rough bar. He has studied many processes of hardening and tempering; he has tools, grinding and polishing wheels, and annealing furnaces. The iron is fused, carbonized into steel, drawn out, forged, tempered, heated white-hot, plunged into cold water or oil to improve its temper, and ground and polished with great care and patience. When this work is done, he shows the astonished blacksmith two thousand dollars' worth of knife-blades where the latter only saw ten dollars' worth of crude horseshoes. The value has been greatly raised by the refining process.

" Knife-blades are all very well, if you can make nothing better," says another artisan, to whom the cutler has shown the triumph of his art, "but you haven't half brought out what is in that bar of iron. I see a higher and better use; I have made a study of iron, and know what there is in it and what can be made of it."

This artisan has a more delicate touch, a finer perception, a better training, a higher ideal, and superior determination, which enable him to look still further into the molecules of the rough bar, past the horseshoes, past the knife-blades, and he turns the crude iron into the finest cambric needles, with eyes cut with microscopic exactness. The production of the invisible points requires a more delicate process, a finer grade of skill than the cutler possesses.

This feat the last workman considers marvelous. He has multiplied many times the value of the cutler's product, and he thinks he has exhausted the possibilities of the iron.

But, behold! another very skillful mechanic, with a still more finely organized mind, a more delicate touch, more patience, more industry, a higher order of skill, and a better training, passes with ease by the horseshoes, the knife blades, and the needles, and returns the product of his bar in fine mainsprings for watches. Where the others saw horseshoes, knife-blades, or needles, worth only a few thousand dollars, his penetrating eye saw a product worth one hundred thousand dollars.

Yet a higher artist-artisan appears, who tells us that the rough bar has not even yet found its highest expression; that he possesses the magic that can perform a still greater miracle in iron. To him even mainsprings seem coarse and clumsy. He knows that the crude iron can be manipulated and coaxed into an elasticity that cannot even be imagined by one less trained in metallurgy. He knows that, if care enough be used in tempering the steel, it will not be stiff, trenchant, and merely a passive metal, but so full of its new qualities that it almost seems instinct with life.

With penetrating, almost clairvoyant vision, this artist-artisan sees how every process of mainspring making can be carried further; and how, at every stage of manufacture, more perfection can be reached; how the texture of the metal can be so much refined that even a fiber, a slender thread of it, can do marvelous work. He puts his bar through many processes of refinement and fine tempering, and in triumph turns his product into almost invisible coils of delicate hairsprings. After infinite toil and pain, he has made his dream true; he has raised the few

132

dollars' worth of iron to a value of one million dollars, perhaps forty times the value of the same weight of gold.

But still another workman, whose processes are so almost infinitely delicate, whose product is so little known by even the average educated man that his trade is unmentioned by the makers of dictionaries and encyclopedias, takes a fragment of one of the bars of steel, and develops its higher possibilities with such marvelous accuracy, such ethereal fineness of touch, that mainsprings and even hairsprings are looked back upon as coarse, crude, and cheap. When his work is done, he shows you a few of the minutely barbed instruments used by dentists to draw out the finest branches of the dental nerves. While a pound of gold, roughly speaking, is worth about two hundred and fifty dollars, a pound of these slender, barbed filaments of steel, if a pound could be collected, might be worth hundreds of times as much.

Other experts may still further refine the product, but it will be many a day before the best will exhaust the possibilities of a metal that can be subdivided until its particles will float in the air. It sounds magical, but the magic is only that wrought by the application of the homeliest virtues; by the training of the eye, the hand, the perception; by painstaking care, by hard work, and by determination and grit.

If a metal possessing only a few coarse material qualities is capable of such marvelous increase in value, by mixing brains with its molecules, who shall set bounds to the possibilities of the development of a human being, that wonderful compound of physical, mental, moral, and spiritual forces? Whereas, in the development of iron, a dozen processes are possible, a thousand influences may be brought to bear upon mind and character. While the iron is an inert mass acted upon by external influences only, the human being is a bundle of forces, acting and counteracting, yet all capable of control and direction by the higher self, the real, dominating personality.

The difference in human attainment is due only slightly to the original material. It is the ideal followed and unfolded, the effort made, the processes of education and experience undergone, that fuse, hammer, and mold our life-bar into its ultimate splendid development.

Life, everyday life, has counterparts of all the tortures the iron undergoes, and through them it comes to its highest expression. The blows of opposition, the struggles amid want and woe, the fiery trials of disaster and bereavement, the crushings of iron circumstances, the raspings of care and anxiety, the grinding of constant difficulties, the rebuffs that chill enthusiasm, the weariness of years of dry, dreary drudgery in education and discipline, all these are necessary to the man who would reach the highest success.

The iron, by this manipulation, is strengthened, refined, made more elastic or more resistant, and adapted to the use of which each artisan dreams. If every blow should fracture it, if every furnace should burn the life out of it, if every roller should pulverize it, of what use would it be? It has that virtue, those qualities that withstand all; that draw profit from every test, and come out triumphant in the end. In the iron the qualities are, in the main, inherent; but in ourselves they are largely matters of growth, culture, and development, and all are subject to the dominating individual will.

Just as each artisan sees in the crude iron some finished, refined product, so must we see in our lives glorious possibilities, if we would but realize them. If we see only horseshoes or knife-blades, all our efforts and struggles will never produce hairsprings. We must realize our own adaptability to great ends; we must resolve to struggle, to endure trials and tests, to pay the necessary price, confident that the result will pay us for our suffering, our trials, and our efforts.

Those who shrink from the forging, the rolling, and the drawing out, are the ones who fail, the" nobodies," the faulty characters, the criminals. Just as a bar of iron, if exposed to the elements, will oxidize, and become worthless, so will character deteriorate if there is no constant effort to improve its form, to increase its ductility, to temper it, or to better it in some way- It is easy to remain a common bar of iron; or comparatively so, by becoming merely a horseshoe; but it is hard to, raise your life product to higher values.

Many of us consider our natural gift-bars poor, mean, and inadequate, compared with those of others; but, if we are willing, by patience, toil, study, and struggle, to hammer, draw out, and refine, to work on and up from clumsy horseshoes to delicate hairsprings, we can, by infinite patience and persistence, raise the value of the raw material to almost fabulous heights. It was thus that Columbus, the weaver, Franklin, the journeyman printer, .Aesop the slave, Homer, the beggar, Demosthenes, the cutler's son, Ben Jonson, the brick layer, Cervantes, the common

134

soldier, and Haydn, the poor wheelwright's son, developed their powers, until they towered head and shoulders above other men.

There is very little difference between the material given to a hundred average boys and girls at birth, yet one with no better means of improvement than the others, perhaps with infinitely poorer means, will raise his material in value a hundredfold, five-hundredfold, aye, a thousandfold, while the ninety-nine will wonder why their material remains so coarse and crude, and will attribute their failure to hard luck.

While one boy is regretting his want of opportunities, his lack of means to get a college education, and remains in ignorance, another with half his chances picks up a good education in the odds and ends of time which other boys throwaway. From the same material, one man builds a palace and another a hovel. From the same rough piece of marble, one man calls out an angel of beauty which delights every beholder, another a hideous monster which demoralizes everyone who sees it.

The extent to which you can raise the value of your life-bar depends upon yourself. Whether you go upward to the mainspring or hairspring stage depends very largely upon your ideal, your determination to be the higher thing, upon your having the grit to be hammered, to be drawn out, to be thrust from the fire into cold water or oil in order to get the proper temper.

Of course, it is hard and painful, and it takes lots of stamina to undergo the processes that produce the finest product, but would you prefer to remain a rough bar of iron or a horseshoe all your life?

14
SELF-IMPROVEMENT THROUGH PUBLIC SPEAKING

IT DOES not matter whether he wants to be a public speaker or not, a person should have such complete control of himself, should be so self-reliant and self-poised, that he can get up in any audience, no matter how large or formidable, and express his thoughts clearly and distinctly.

Self-expression in some manner is the only means of developing mental power. It may be in music; it may be on canvas; it may he through oratory; it may come through selling goods or writing a book; but it must come through self-expression.

Self-expression in any legitimate form tends to call out what is in a man, his resourcefulness, inventiveness; but no other form of self-expression develops a man so thoroughly and so effectively, and so quickly unfolds all of his powers, as speaking before an audience.

It is doubtful whether anyone can reach the highest standard of culture without studying the art of expression, especially public vocal expression. In all ages oratory has been regarded as the highest expression of human achievement. Young people, no matter what they intend to be, whether blacksmith or farmer, merchant or physician, should make it a study.

Nothing else will call out what is in a man so quickly and so effectively as the constant effort to do his best in speaking before an audience. When one undertakes to think on his feet and speak extemporaneously before the public, the power and the skill of the entire man are put to a severe test.

The practise of public speaking, the effort to marshal all one's forces in a logical and forceful manner,· to bring to a focus all the power one possesses, is a great awakener of all the faculties. The sense of power that comes from holding the attention, stirring the emotions, or convincing the reason of an audience, gives self-confidence, assurance, self-reliance, arouses ambition and tends to make one more effective in every way.

One's judgment, education, manhood, character, all the things that go to make a man what he is, are being unrolled like a panorama in his effort to express himself. Every mental faculty is quickened, every power of thought and expression stirred and spurred. The speaker summons all his reserves of experience, of knowledge, of natural or acquired ability, and masses all his forces in the endeavor to express himself with power and to capture the approval and applause of his audience.

A writer has the advantage of being able to wait for his moods. He can write when he feels like it; and he knows that he can burn his manuscript again and again if it does not suit him. There are not a thousand eyes upon him. He does not have a great audience criticizing every sentence, weighing every thought. He does not have to step upon the scales of every listener's judgment to be weighed, as does the orator. He may write as listlessly as he pleases, use much or little of his brain or energy, just as he chooses or feels like doing. No one is watching him. His pride and vanity are not touched, and what he writes may never be seen by anyone. Then, there is always a chance for revision. In music, whether vocal or instrumental, what one gives out is only partially one's own; the rest is the composer's. In conversation, we do not feel that so much de- pends upon our words; only a few persons hear them, and perhaps no one will ever think of them again. But when a person attempts to speak before an audience, all props are knocked out from under him; he has nothing to lean upon, he can get no assistance, no advice; he must find all his resources in *himself;* he stands absolutely alone. He may have millions of money, broad acres of land, and may live in a palace, but none of these avail him now; his memory, his experience, his education, his ability, are all he has; he must be measured by what he says, what he reveals of himself in his speech; he must stand or fall in the estimation of his audience.

Anyone who lays any claim to culture should train himself to think on his feet, so that he can at a moment's notice rise and express himself intelligently. The occasions for after-dinner speaking are increasing enormously. A great many questions which once were settled in the office are now discussed and disposed of at dinners. All sorts of business deals are now carried through at dinners. There was never before any such demand for dinner oratory as to-day.

We know men who have, by dint of hard work and persistent grit, lifted themselves into positions of prominence, and yet they are not able to stand on their feet in public, even to make a few remarks or to put a motion, without trembling like an aspen leaf. They had plenty of opportunities when they were young, at school, in debating clubs, to get rid of their self-consciousness and to acquire ease and facility in public speaking, but they always shrank from every opportunity, because they were timid, or felt that somebody else could handle the debate or questions better.

There are plenty of business men to-day who would give a great deal of money if they could only go back and improve the early opportunities for learning to think and speak on their feet which they threw away. Now they have money, they have position, but they are nobodies when called upon to speak in public. All they can do is to look foolish, blush, stammer out an apology, and sit down.

Some time ago I was at a public meeting when a man who stands very high in the community, who is king in his specialty, was called upon to give his opinion upon the matter under consideration, and he got up and trembled and stammered and could scarcely say his soul was his own. He could not even make a decent appearance. He had power and a great deal of experience, but there he stood, as helpless as a child, and he felt cheap, mortified, embarrassed. Probably he would have given anything if he had early in life trained himself to speak extemporaneously, so that he could think on his feet and say with power and effectiveness that which he knew.

At the very meeting where this strong man, who had the respect and confidence of everybody who knew him, had made such a miserable failure of his attempt to give his opinion upon the important public matter on which he was well posted, a shallow-brained business man of the same city who hadn't a hundredth part of the other man's practical power in affairs, got up and made a brilliant speech, and strangers no doubt thought that he was much the stronger man. He had simply cultivated the ability to say his best thing on his feet, and the other man had not.

A brilliant young man in New York who has climbed to a responsible position in a very short time, tells me that he has been surprised on several occasions when he has been called upon to speak at banquets, or at other public functions, at the new discoveries he has made of himself of power which he never before dreamed he possessed, and he now regrets more than anything else that he has in the past allowed so many opportunities for calling himself out to go by.

The effort to express one's ideas in lucid, clean-cut, concise, telling English tends to make one's everyday language choicer and more direct, and to improve one's diction generally. In this and other ways speech-making develops mental power and character. This explains the rapidity with which a young man develops in school or college when he begins to take part in public debates or in debating societies.

Every man, says Lord Chesterfield, may choose good words instead of bad ones and speak properly instead of improperly; he may have grace in his motions and gestures, and may be a very agreeable instead of disagreeable speaker if he will take care and pains.

It is a matter of painstaking and preparation. There is everything in learning what you wish to know. Your vocal culture, manner, and mental furnishing, are to be made a matter for thought and careful training.

In thinking on one's feet before an audience, one must think quickly, vigorously, effectively. At the same time he must speak through a properly modulated voice, with proper facial and bodily expression and gesture. This requires practise in early life.

Nothing will tire an audience more quickly than monotony, everything expressed on the same dead level. There must be variety; the human mind tires very quickly when this is not supplied.

This is especially true of a monotonous tone. It is a great art to be able to raise and lower the voice with sweet flowing cadences which please the ear. Gladstone said, "Ninety-nine men in every hundred never rise above mediocrity because the training of the voice is entirely neglected and considered of no importance."

It was said of a certain Duke of Devonshire that he was the only English statesman who ever took a nap during the progress of his own speech. He was a perfect genius for dry, uninteresting oratory, moving forward with a monotonous droning, and pausing now and then as if refreshing himself by slumber.

In youth the would-be orator must cultivate robust health, since force, enthusiasm, conviction, will-power are greatly affected by physical condition; and, too, he must cultivate bodily posture, and have good habits at easy command. 'What would have been the result of Webster's reply to Hayne, the greatest oratorical effort ever made on this continent, if he had sat down in the Senate and put his feet on his desk? Think of a great singer like Nordica attempting to electrify an audience while lounging on a sofa or sitting in a slouchy position!

There is no class of people put to such a severe test of showing what is in them as public speakers; no other men who run such a risk of exposing their weak spots, or making fools of themselves in the estimation of others, as do orators. Public speaking-thinking on one's feet is a powerful educator except to the thick-skinned man, the man who has no sensitiveness, or who does not care for what others think of him. Nothing else so thoroughly discloses a man's weaknesses or shows up his limitations of thought, his poverty of speech, his narrow vocabulary; nothing else is such a touchstone of character and the extent of one's reading, the carefulness or carelessness of his observation as his public utterances.

An early training for effective speaking will make one careful to secure a good vocabulary by good reading and a dictionary. One must know words.

Close, compact statement is imperative, Learn to stop when you get through. Do not keep stringing out conversation or argument after you have made your point. You only neutralize the good impression you have made, weaken your case, and prejudice people against you for your lack of tact, good judgment, or sense of proportion.

The attempt to become a good public speaker is a great awakener of all the mental faculties. The sense of power that comes from holding the attention, stirring the emotions or convincing the reason of an audience, gives self-confidence, assurance, self-reliance, arouses ambition, and tends to make one more effective in every particular. One's manhood, character, learning, judgment of his opinions all things that go to make him what he is-are being unrolled like a panorama. Every mental faculty is quickened, every power of thought and expression spurred. Thoughts rush for utterance, words press for choice. The speaker summons all his reserves of education, of experience, of natural or acquired ability, and masses all his forces in the endeavor to capture the approval and applause of the audience.

Such an effort takes hold of the entire nature, beads the brow, fires the eye, flushes the cheek, and sends the blood surging through the veins. Dormant impulses are stirred, half-forgotten memories revived, the imagination quickened to see figures and similes that would never come to calm thought.

This forced awakening of the whole personality has effects reaching much further than the oratorical occasion. The effort to marshal all one's reserves in a logical and orderly manner, to bring to the front all the power one possesses, leaves these reserves permanently better in hand, more readily in reach.

The Debating Club is the nursery of orators. No matter how far you have to go to attend it, or how much trouble it is, or how difficult it is to get the time, the drill you will get by it is often the turning point. Lincoln, Wilson, Webster, Choate, Clay, and Patrick Henry got their training in the old-fashioned Debating Society.

Do not think that because you do not know anything about parliamentary law you should not accept the presidency of your club or debating society, or take an active part. This is just the place to learn, and when you have accepted the position you can post yourself on the rules, and the chances are that you will never know the rules until you are thrust into the chair where you will be obliged to give rulings. Join just as many young people's organizations-especially self-improvement organizations-as you can, and force yourself to speak every time you get a chance. If the chance does not come to you, make it. Jump to your feet and say something upon every question that is up for discussion. Do not be afraid to rise to put a motion or to second it or to give your opinion upon it. Do not wait until you are better prepared. You never will be.

Every time you rise to your feet will increase your confidence, and after a while you will form the habit of speaking until it will be as easy as anything else. There is no one thing which will develop young people so rapidly and effectively as debating clubs and discussions of all sorts. A vast number of our public men have owed their advance more to the old-fashioned debating societies than anything else. Here they learned confidence, self-reliance; they discovered themselves. It was here they learned not to be afraid of themselves, to express their opinions with force and independence. Nothing will call a young man out more than the struggle to hold his own in a debate. It is strong, vigorous exercise for the mind just as wrestling is for the body.

Do not remain way back on the rear seat. Go up front. Do not be afraid to show yourself. This shrinking into a corner and getting out of sight and avoiding publicity is fatal to self-confidence.

It is so easy and tempting, especially for boys and girls in school or college, to shrink from the public debates or speaking, on the ground that they are not quite well enough educated at present. They want to wait until they can use a little better grammar, until they have read more history and more literature, until they have gained a little more culture and ease of manner.

But the way to acquire grace, ease, facility, the way to get poise and balance so that you will not feel disturbed in public gatherings, is to get the *experience*. Do the thing so many times that it will become second nature to you. If you have an invitation to speak, no matter how much you may shrink from it, or how timid or shy you may be, resolve that you will not let this opportunity for self enlargement slip by you.

I know of a young man who has a great deal of natural ability for public speaking, and yet he is so timid that he always shrinks from accepting invitations to speak at banquets or in public because he is so afraid that he has not had experience enough. He lacks confidence in himself, He is so proud, and so afraid that he will make some slip which will mortify him, that he has waited and waited and waited until now he is discouraged and thinks that he will never be able to do anything in public speaking at all. He would give anything in the world if he had only accepted all of the invitations he has had, because then he would have profited by experience. It would have been a thousand times better for him to have made a mistake, or even to have broken down entirely a few times, than to have missed the scores of opportunities which would undoubtedly have made a strong public speaker of him.

What is technically called "stage fright" is very common. A college boy recited an address" To the conscript fathers." His professor asked,-" Is that the way Caesar would have spoken it?" " Yes," he replied, "if Caesar had been scared half to death, and as nervous as a cat."

An almost fatal timidity seizes on an inexperienced person when he knows that all eyes are watching him, that everybody in his audience is

142

trying to measure and weigh him, studying him, scrutinizing him to see how much there is in him, for what he stands, and making up their minds whether he measures more or less than they expected.

Some men are constitutionally sensitive and so afraid of being gazed at that they don't dare open their mouths, even when a question in which they are deeply interested and on which they have strong views is being discussed. At debating clubs, meetings of literary societies, or gatherings of any kind, they sit dumb, longing, yet fearing to speak. The sound of their own voices, if they should get on their feet to make a motion or to speak in a public gathering, would paralyze them. The mere thought of asserting themselves, of putting forward their views or opinions on any subject as being worthy of attention, or as valuable as those of their companions, makes them blush and shrink more into themselves.

This timidity is often, however, not so much the fear of one's audience, as the fear lest one can make no suitable expression of his thought.

The hardest thing for the public speaker to overcome is self-consciousness. Those terrible eyes which pierce him through and through, which are measuring him, criticizing him, are very difficult to get out of his consciousness.

But no orator can make a great impression until he gets rid of himself, until he can absolutely annihilate his self-consciousness, forget himself in his speech. While he is wondering what kind of an impression he is making, what people think of him, his power is crippled, and his speech to that extent will be mechanical, wooden.

Even a partial failure on the platform has good results, for it often arouses a determination to conquer the next time, which never leaves one. Demosthenes' heroic efforts, and Disraeli's "The time will come when you will hear me," are historic examples.

It is not the speech, but the man behind the speech, that wins a way to the front.

One man carries weight because he is himself the embodiment of power, he is himself convinced of what he says. There is nothing of the negative, the doubtful, the uncertain in his nature. He not only knows a thing, but he knows that he knows it. His opinion carries with it the entire weight of his being. The whole man gives consent to his judgment. He himself is in his conviction, in his act.

One of the most entrancing speakers I have ever listened to--a man to hear whom people would go long distances and stand for hours to get admission to the hall where he spoke never was able to get the confidence of his audience because he lacked character. People liked to be swayed by his eloquence. There was a great charm in the cadences of his perfect sentences. But somehow they could not believe what he said.

The orator must be sincere. The public is very quick to see through shams. If the audience sees mud at the bottom of your eye, that you are not honest yourself, that you are acting, they will not take any stock in you.

It is not enough to say a pleasing thing, an interesting thing, the orator must be able to convince; and to convince others he must himself have strong convictions.

Very few people ever rise to their greatest possibilities or ever know their entire power unless confronted by some great occasion. We are as much amazed as others are when, in some great emergency, we out-do ourselves. Somehow the power that stands behind us in the silence, in the depths of our natures, comes to our relief, intensifies our faculties a thousandfold and enables us to do things which before we thought impossible.

It would be difficult to estimate the great part which practical drill in oratory may play in one's life.

Great occasions, when nations have been in peril, have developed and brought out some of the greatest orators of the world. Cicero, Mirabeau, Patrick Henry, Webster, and John Bright might all be called to witness to this fact.

The occasion had much to do with the greatest speech delivered in the United States Senate: Webster's reply to Hayne. Webster had no time for immediate preparation, but the occasion brought out all the reserves in this giant, and he towered so far above his opponent that Hayne looked like a pygmy in comparison.

The pen has discovered many a genius, but the process is slower and less effective than the great occasion that discovers the orator.

Every crisis calls out ability previously undeveloped and perhaps unsuspected.

No orator living was ever great enough to give out the same power and force and magnetism to an empty hall, to empty seats, that he could give to an audience capable of being fired by his theme. In the presence of the audience lies a fascination, an indefinable magnetism that stimulates all the mental faculties, and acts as a tonic and vitalizer. An orator can say before an audience what he could not possibly have said before he went on the platform, just as we can often say to a friend in animated conversation things which we could not possibly say when alone. As when two chemicals are united, a new substance is formed from the combination which did not exist in either alone, he feels surging through his brain the combined force of his audience, which he calls inspiration, a mighty power which did not exist in his own personality.

Actors tell us that there is an indescribable inspiration which comes from the orchestra, the footlights, the audience, which it is impossible to feel at a cold mechanical rehearsal. There is something in a great sea of expectant faces which awakens the ambition and arouses the reserve of power which can never be felt except before an audience. The power was there just the same before, but it was not aroused.

In the presence of a great orator, the audience is absolutely in his power. They laugh or cry as he pleases, or rise and fall at his bidding, until he releases them from the magic spell.

What is oratory but to stir the blood of all hearers, to so arouse their emotions that they cannot control themselves a moment longer without taking the action to which they are impelled?

"His words are laws" may: be well said of the statesman whose orations sway the world. What art is greater than that of changing the minds of men?

Wendell Phillips so played upon the emotions, so changed the convictions of Southerners who hated him, but who were curious to listen to his oratory, that for the time being he almost persuaded them that they were in the wrong. I have seen him when it seemed to me that he was almost godlike in his power. With the ease of a master he swayed his audience. Some who hated him in the slavery days were there, and they could not resist cheering him.

When James Russell Lowell was a student, said Wetmore Story, he and Story went to Faneuil Hall to hear Webster. They meant to hoot him for his remaining in Tyler's cabinet. It would be easy, they reasoned, to get the three thousand people to join them. When he began, Lowell turned pale, and Story livid. His great eyes, they thought, were fixed on them. His opening words changed their scorn to admiration, and their contempt to respect.

"He gave us a glimpse into the Holy of Holies," said another student, in relating his experience in -listening to a great preacher.

15
WHAT A GOOD APPEARANCE WILL DO

The apparel oft proclaims the man. SHAKESPEARE.

As a general thing an individual who is neat in his person is neat in his morals.-H. W. SHAW.

THERE are two chief factors in good appearance; cleanliness of body and comeliness of attire. Usually these go together, neatness of attire indicating a sanitary care of the person, while outward slovenliness suggests a carelessness of appearance that probably goes deeper than the clothes covering the body.

We express ourselves first of all in our bodies. The outer condition of the body is accepted as the symbol of the inner. If it is unlovely, or repulsive, through sheer neglect or indifference, we conclude that the mind corresponds with it. As a rule, the conclusion is a just one. High ideals and strong, clean, wholesome lives and work are incompatible with low standards of personal cleanliness. A young man who neglects his bath will neglect his mind; he will quickly deteriorate in every way. A young woman who ceases to care for her appearance in minutest detail will soon cease to please. She will fall little by little until she degenerates into an ambitionless slattern.

It is not to be wondered at that the Talmud places cleanliness next to godliness. I should place it nearer still, for I believe that absolute cleanliness *is* godliness. Cleanliness or purity of soul and body raises man to the highest estate. Without this he is nothing but a brute. There is a very close connection between a fine, strong, clean physique and a fine, strong, clean character. A man who allows himself to become careless in regard to the one will, in spite of himself, fall away in the other.

But self-interest clamors as loudly as esthetic or moral considerations for the fulfillment of the laws of cleanliness. Every day we see people receiving "demerits" for failure to live up to them. I can recall instances of capable stenographers who forfeited their positions because they did not keep their finger nails clean. An honest, intelligent man whom I know lost his place in a large publishing firm because he was careless about shaving and caring for his teeth. Not very long since a lady remarked that she went into a store to buy some ribbons, but when she saw the salesgirl's hands she changed her mind and made her purchase elsewhere. "Dainty ribbons," she said, "could not be handled by such soiled fingers without losing some of their freshness." Of course, it will not be long until that girl's employer will discover that she is not advancing his business, and then, well, the law will work inexorably.

The first point to be emphasized in the making of a good appearance is the necessity of frequent bathing. A daily bath insures a clean, wholesome condition of the skin, without which health is impossible.

Next in importance to the bath is the proper care of the hair, the hands, and the teeth. This requires little more than a small amount of time and the use of soap and water.

Manicure sets are so cheap that they are within the reach of almost everyone. If you cannot afford to buy a whole set, you can buy a file and keep your nails smooth and clean.

Keeping the teeth in good condition is a very simple matter, yet perhaps more people sin in this particular point of cleanliness than in any other. I know young men, and young women, too, who dress very well and seem to take considerable pride in their personal appearance, yet neglect their teeth. They do not realize that there could hardly be a worse blot on one's appearance than dirty or decaying teeth, or the absence of one or two in front. Nothing can be more offensive in man or woman than a foul breath, and no one can have neglected teeth without reaping this consequence. No employer wants a clerk, or stenographer, whose appearance is marred by a lack of one or two front teeth. Many an applicant has been denied the position he sought because of bad teeth.

For those who have to make their way in the world, the best counsel on the subject of clothes may be summed up in this short sentence, "Let thy attire be comely, but not costly." Simplicity in dress is its greatest charm, and in these days, when there is such an infinite variety of tasteful but inexpensive fabrics to choose from, the majority can afford to be well dressed. But no one need blush for a shabby suit, if circumstances prevent his having a better one. You will be more respected by yourself and everyone else with an old coat on your back that has been paid for than a new one that has not. It is not the shabbiness that is unavoidable, but the slovenliness that is avoidable, that the world frowns upon. If you are dressed according to your means, no matter how poorly, you are appropriately dressed. The consciousness of making the best appearance you possibly can, of always being scrupulously neat and clean, and of maintaining your self-respect and integrity at all costs, will sustain you under the most adverse circumstances, and give you a dignity, strength, and magnetic forcefulness that will command the respect and admiration of others.

Herbert H. Vreeland, who rose in a short time from a section hand on the Long Island Railroad to the presidency of all the surface railways in New York City, in the course of an address on how to attain success, said: "Clothes don't make the man, but good clothes have got many a man a good job. If you have twenty-five dollars, and want a job, it is better to spend twenty dollars for a suit of clothes, four dollars for shoes, and the rest for a shave, a hair-cut, and a clean collar, and walk to the place, than go with the money in the pockets of a dingy suit."

Most large business houses make it a rule not to employ anyone who looks seedy, or slovenly, or who does not make a good appearance when he applies for a position. The man who hires all the salespeople for one of the largest retail stores in Chicago says: "While the routine of application is in every case strictly adhered to, the fact remains that the most important element in an applicant's chance for a trial is his personality."

It does not matter how much merit or ability an applicant for a position may possess, he cannot afford to be careless of his personal appearance. Diamonds in the rough of infinitely greater value than the polished glass of some of those who get positions may, occasionally, be rejected. Applicants whose good appearance helped them to secure a place may often be very superficial in comparison with some who were rejected in their favor; but having secured it, they may keep it, though not possessing half the ability of the man or woman who was turned away.

That the same rule that governs employers in America holds in England, is evidenced by the" London Draper's Record." It says:-"Wherever a marked personal care is exhibited for the cleanliness of the person and for neatness in dress, there is also almost always found extra carefulness as regards the finish of work done. Work people whose personal habits are slovenly produce slovenly work; those who are careful of their own appearance are equally careful of the looks of the work they turn out. And probably what is true of the workroom is equally true of the region behind the counter. Is it not a fact that the smart saleswoman is usually rather particular about her dress, is averse to wearing dingy collars, frayed cuffs, and faded ties? The truth of the matter seems to be that extra care as regards personal habits and general appearance is, as a rule, indicative of a certain alertness of mind, which shows itself antagonistic to slovenliness of all kind."

No young man or woman who wishes to retain that most potent factor of the successful life, self-respect, can afford to be negligent in the matter of dress, for" the character is subdued to what it is clothed in." As the consciousness of being well dressed tends to grace and ease of manner, so shabby, ill-fitting, or soiled attire makes one feel awkward and constrained, lacking in dignity and importance. Our clothes unmistakably affect our feelings and self-respect, as anyone knows who has experienced the sensation and who has not? that comes from being attired in new and becoming raiment. Poor, ill-fitting, or soiled garments are detrimental to morals and manners. "The consciousness of clean linen," says Elizabeth Stuart Phelps, "is in and of itself a source of moral strength, second only to that of a clean conscience. A well ironed collar or a fresh glove has carried many a man through an emergency in which a wrinkle or a rip would have defeated him." The importance of attending to little details the perfection of which really constitutes the well-dressed man or woman is well illustrated by this story of a young woman's failure to secure a desirable position. One of those large-souled women of wealth, in which our generation is rich, had established an industrial school for girls in which they received a good English education and were trained to be self-supporting. She needed the services of a superintendent and teacher, and considered herself fortunate when the trustees of the institution recommended to her a young woman whose tact, knowledge, perfect manners, and general fitness for the position they extolled in the highest terms. The young woman was invited by the founder of the school to call on her at once. Apparently she possessed all the required qualifications; and yet, without assigning any reason, Mrs. V. absolutely refused to give her a trial. Long afterward, when questioned by a friend as to the cause of her seemingly inexplicable conduct in refusing to engage so competent a teacher, she replied: "It was a trifle, but a trifle in which, as in an Egyptian hieroglyphic, lay a volume of meaning. The young woman came to me fashionably and expensively dressed, but with torn and soiled gloves, and half of the buttons off her shoes. A slovenly woman is not a fit guide for any young girl." Probably the applicant never knew why she did not obtain the position, for she was undoubtedly well qualified to fill it in every respect, except in this seemingly unimportant matter of attention to the little details of dress.

From every point of view it pays well to dress well. The knowledge that we are becomingly clothed acts like a mental tonic. Very few men or women are so strong and so perfectly poised as to be unaffected by their surroundings. If you lie around half-dressed, without making your toilet, and with your room all in disorder, taking it easy because you do not expect or wish to see anybody, you will find yourself very quickly taking on the mood of your attire and environment. Your mind will slip down; it will refuse to exert itself; it will become as slovenly, slipshod, and inactive as your body. On the other hand, if, when you have an attack of the "blues," when you feel half sick and not able to work, instead of lying around the house in your old wrapper or dressing gown, you take a good bath, a Turkish bath, if you can afford it, put on your best clothes, and make your toilet as carefully as if you were going to a fashionable reception, you will feel like a new person. Nine times out of ten before you have finished dressing your " blues" and your half-sick feeling will have vanished like a bad dream, and your whole outlook on life will have changed.

By emphasizing the importance of dress I do not mean that you should be like Beau Brummel, the English fop, who spent four thousand dollars a year at his tailor's alone, and who used to take hours to tie his cravat. An undue love of dress is worse than a total disregard of it, and they love dress too much who, like Beau Brummel, devote most of their chief object in life to the neglect of their most sacred duty to themselves and others, or who, like Beau Brummel, devote most of their waking hours to its study. But I do claim, in view of its effect on ourselves and on those with whom we come in contact, that it is a duty, as well as the truest economy, to dress as well and becomingly as our position requires and our means will allow.

Many young men and women make the mistake of thinking that "well dressed" necessarily means being expensively dressed, and, with this erroneous idea in mind, they fall into as great a pitfall as those who think clothes are of no importance. They devote the time that should be given to the culture of head and heart to studying their toilets, and planning how they can buy, out of their limited salaries, this or that expensive hat, or tie, or coat, which they see exhibited in some fashionable store. If they cannot by any possibility afford the coveted article, they buy some cheap, tawdry imitation, the effect of which is only to make them look ridiculous. Young men of this stamp wear cheap rings, vermilion tinted ties, and broad checks, and almost invariably they occupy cheap positions. Like the dandy, whom Carlyle describes as "a clothes-wearing man, a man whose trade, office, and existence consists in the wearing of clothes, every faculty of whose soul, spirit, person, and purse is heroically consecrated to this One object," they live to dress, and have no time to devote to self-culture or to fitting themselves for higher positions.

The overdressed young woman is merely the feminine of the overdressed young man. The manners of both seem to have a subtle connection with their clothes. They are loud, flashy, vulgar. Their style of dress bespeaks a type of character even more objectionable than that of the slovenly, untidily dressed person. The world accepts the truth announced by Shakespeare that "the apparel oft proclaims the man"; and the man and the woman, too, are frequently condemned by the very garb which they think makes them so irresistible. At first sight, it may seem hasty or superficial to judge men or women by their clothes, but experience has proved, again and again, that they do, as a rule, measure the sense and self-respect of the wearer; and aspirants to success should be as careful in choosing their dress as their companions. The old adage: "Tell me thy company and I will tell thee what thou art," is offset by this wise saying of some philosopher of the commonplace: "Show me all' the dresses a woman has worn in the course of her life, and I will write you her biography."

"How exquisitely absurd it is," says Sydney Smith, "to teach a girl that beauty is of no value, dress of no use. Beauty is of value. Her whole prospect and happiness in life may often depend upon a new gown or a becoming bonnet. If she has five grains of common sense, she will find this out. The great thing is to teach her their proper value."

It is true that clothes do not make the man, but they have a much larger influence on man's life than we are wont to attribute to them. Prentice Mulford declares dress to be one of the avenues for the spiritualization of the race. This is not an extravagant statement, when we remember what an effect clothes have in inciting to personal cleanliness. Let a woman, for instance, don an old soiled or worn wrapper, and it will have the effect of making her indifferent as to whether her hair is frowsy or in curl papers. It does not matter whether her face and hands are clean or not, or what sort of slipshod shoes she wears, for "anything," she argues, "is good enough to go with this old wrapper." Her walk, her manner, the general trend of her feelings, will in some subtle way be dominated by the old wrapper. Suppose she changes, puts on a dainty muslin garment instead; how different her looks and acts! Her hair must be becomingly arranged, so as not to be at odds with her dress. Her face and hands and finger nails must be spotless as the muslin which surrounds them. The down-at-heel old shoes are exchanged for suitable slippers. Her mind runs along new channels. She has much more respect for the wearer of the new, clean wrapper than for the wearer of the old, soiled one. "Would you change the current of your thoughts? Change your raiment, and you will at once feel the effect." Even so great an authority as Buffon, the naturalist and philosopher, testifies to the influence of dress on thought. He declared himself utterly incapable of thinking to good purpose except in full court dress. This he always put on before entering his study, not even omitting his sword.

There is something about ill-fitting, unbecoming, or shabby apparel which not only robs one of self-respect, but also of comfort and power. Good clothes give ease of manner, and make one talk well. The' consciousness of being well dressed gives a grace and ease of manner that even religion will not bestow, while inferiority of garb often induces restraint.

One cannot but feel that God is a lover of appropriate dress. He has put robes of beauty and glory upon all His works. Every flower is dressed in richness; every field blushes beneath a mantle of beauty; every star is veiled in brightness; every bird is clothed in the habiliments of the most exquisite taste. And surely He is pleased when we provide a beautiful setting for the greatest of His handiworks.

16
SELF-RELIANCE

A normal person is capable of independence and self-reliance, yet comparatively few people ever develop their ability to stand alone. It is so much easier to lean, to trail, to follow somebody else, to let others do the thinking and the planning and the work.

One of the worst faults of the typical American is that, if he does not possess commanding talents in some particular direction, he usually does not think it worthwhile to make the most of what he has.

Do not think that, just because you are not a born leader, you are a born leaner. Because you have no great commanding qualities of leadership is no reason why you should not cultivate the little you have. We never know what resources or possibilities of strength are ours until we put our powers to the test. Many a man has proved himself a great leader who did not seem to be so naturally who showed at first very little evidence of self-reliance.

Leaders do not copy. They do not reflect the opinion of the majority. They think. They create. They make their own program and carry it out.

How few people stand for anything in particular! The majority of mankind are merely so many individuals in the census; they help make a little larger crowd; but how few men stand above or beyond their fellows and are self-sufficient!

Almost everybody you see is leaning on something or somebody. Some lean on their money, some on their friends; some depend upon their clothes, their pedigree, their social standing; but how seldom we see a man who stands fair and square on his own feet; who goes through life on his own merits, and is self-reliant and resourceful.

In later life we never quite forgive those who have allowed us to lean upon them, for we know that it has deprived us of our birthright.

A child is not satisfied when his father shows him how to do a certain thing. But watch the exultant expression on his face when by actually doing it he has conquered the thing himself. This new sense of conquest is an added power which increases self-confidence and self-respect.

A college education does not develop the practical faculties. It merely furnishes the workman with his tools. He must learn by practise how to wield them skillfully. It is the school of "hard knocks" that develops character and brings out the success material in a man.

Henry Ward Beecher used to tell the following story of how he was taught, when a boy, to depend on himself:

"I was sent to the blackboard, and went, uncertain, full of whimpering.

"'That lesson must be learned,' said my teacher, in a quiet tone, but with terrible intensity. All explanations and excuses he trod under foot with utter scornfulness. 'I want that problem; I don't want any reason why you haven't it,' he would say.

"'I did study two hours.'

"'That's nothing to me; I want the lesson. You need not study it at all, or you may study it, ten hours, just to suit yourself. I want the lesson.'

"It was tough for a green boy, but it seasoned me. In less than a month, I had the most intense sense of intellectual independence and courage to defend my recitations.

"One day his cold, calm voice fell upon me in the midst of a demonstration, 'No "I hesitated, and then went back to the beginning; and, when I reached the same point again, 'No!' uttered in a tone of conviction, barred my progress.

"The next!' I sat down in red confusion. "He, too, was stopped with' No!' but went right on, and finished; and, 'as he sat down, was rewarded with ' Very well.' " , Why,' whimpered I, ' I recited it just as he did, and you said" No! " , " 'Why didn't you say "Yes," and stick to it? "It is not enough to know your lesson; you must know that you know it. You have learned nothing until you are sure. If all the world says " No," your business is to say " Yes," and prove it.' "

The greatest service a teacher can render a pupil is to train him to depend upon himself, to trust to his own powers. If the youth does not practise self-reliance, the man will be a weakling, a failure.

One of the greatest delusions that a human being could ever have is that he is permanently benefited by continued assistance from others.

Power is the goal of every worthy ambition, and only weakness comes from imitation or dependence on others. Power is self-developed, self-generated. We cannot increase the strength of our muscles by sitting in a gymnasium and letting another exercise for us. Nothing else so destroys the power to stand alone as the habit of leaning upon others. If you lean, you will never be strong or original. Stand alone or bury your ambition to be somebody in the world. The man who tries to give his children a start in the world so that they will not have to struggle as hard as he had to, is unknowingly bringing disaster upon them. What he calls giving them a start will probably give them a setback in the world. Young people need all the motive power they can get. They are naturally leaners, imitators, copiers, and it is easy for them to develop into echoes, imitations. They will not walk alone while you furnish crutches; they will lean upon you just as long as you will let them.

It is self-help, not pulls or influence, self-reliance, not leaning upon others, that develops stamina and strength.

"He who sits on the cushion of advantage goes to sleep," said Emerson.

What is there so paralyzing to strenuous endeavor, so fatal to self-exertion, to self-help, as to be helped, as to feel that there is no necessity for exertion because somebody else has done everything for us!

"One of the most disgusting sights in the world is that of a young man with healthy blood, broad shoulders, a presentable pair of calves, and one hundred and fifty pounds more or less of bone and muscle, standing with his hands in his pockets longing for help."

Did you ever think how many of the people you know are just waiting for something? Many of them do not know just what; but they are waiting for something. They have an indefinite idea that somehow something is coming to them, that there will be some fortunate conjunction of circumstances, or something will happen which will make an opening for them, or someone will help them, so that without very great education or preparation or capital, they can get a start for themselves, or get ahead some way.

Some are waiting for money which may come from a father's fortune, from a rich uncle, or some other distant relative. Others are waiting for that mysterious something called "luck," a "pull" or a "boost" to help them.

I have never known a person who had this habit of waiting for help, or for somebody to give him a boost, of waiting for somebody's money, or for assistance of any kind, or for luck to come to him, that never really amounted to much.

It is the man who strips himself of every prop, who throws away his crutches, burns his bridges behind him, and depends upon himself, that wins. Self-reliance is the key that opens the door to achievement. Self-reliance is the unfolder of power.

There is nothing that will so undermine self-confidence, which is the very foundation stone of all achievement, as the habit of expecting help from others.

A man at the head of a large company recently said that he was trying to place his son in another business house, where he would get hard knocks. He did not want him to start with him because he was afraid he might lean on him or expect favors.

Boys who are pampered by their fathers, allowed to come to business at all sorts of hours, to leave when they please, and to remain away when they feel like it, rarely amount to much. It is the development of self-reliance that gives strength and confidence. Depending on oneself is what develops the power of achievement, the ability to do things.

It is a dangerous thing to put a boy where he can lean on his father or expect favors. It is a difficult thing to learn to swim in shallow water, where one knows he can touch bottom. A boy will learn a great deal quicker where the water is over his head, where he is compelled to swim or sink. When he has cut off all chances for retreat he will reach the shore safely. It is human nature to lean when possible, not to do a thing until we feel the spur of necessity. It is the "must" in our lives that brings out the best thing in us.

This is why boys who never amount to much at home, when they are always helped by their fathers, often develop marvelous ability in a very short time when they are thrown upon their own resources, when they are obliged to do, or bear the disgrace of failure.

The moment you give up trying to get help from others, and become independent and self-reliant, you will start on the road to success. The moment you throw overboard all help outside of yourself, you will develop strength you never before realized you possessed.

There is nothing so valuable in this world as your own self-respect; and you cannot keep this if you go from one person to another trying to get help. You will be an infinitely stronger man or woman if you will just make up your mind that you are going to rely upon yourself, that you will put yourself in a position of independence.

Outside help may seem to you a blessing at times; but it is usually a curse because of its crippling power. People who give you money are not your best friends. Your friends are those who urge you, who force you to depend upon yourself, to help yourself.

There are plenty of people older than you are, with only one leg or one arm, who manage to earn a living, while you who are healthy and physically able to work are looking to others for assistance. No able-bodied person can feel that he is quite a man while he is dependent. When one has a trade, a profession, or some kind of occupation which makes him absolutely independent, he feels a sense of added power, resourcefulness, completeness, which nothing else can give. Responsibility discovers ability. Many a youth discovers himself for the first time when he goes into business for himself. He might have worked for years for somebody else without ever finding himself.

It is not possible to develop one's utmost possibilities while working for somebody else.

There is not the motive, the same reach of ambition or enthusiasm. No matter how conscientious to duty, there is not the same stimulus or incentive to bring out the possible man that God intended. The best in a man is his independence, his self-reliance, his originality, and these will never reach their highest expression under service to somebody else while human nature remains what it is now.

It does not take a great amount of skill, a long experience in seamanship, to steer a ship in a calm. It is when the ocean is lashed into fury by the tempest; it is when the ship is plowing through the trough of the sea which threatens to engulf it; when everybody else is terrified; when there is a panic on board among the passengers and when the crew is in mutiny, that the captain's seamanship is tested.

It is only when the brain is tested to its utmost, when every bit of ingenuity and sagacity a young man possesses must come to the rescue of a possible failure, that he will develop his greatest strength. It takes months and years of effort to stretch small capital over a larger business without disaster. It is the perpetual struggle to keep up appearances, to get and to hold customers, that will call out the reserve in a young man. It is when money is scarce and business dull, and living high, that the real man is making his greatest progress. Where there is no struggle, there is no growth, no character.

What are the chances of a youth developing his own innate resources who knows he has money enough to buy his" education" and need not work for it, and who pays a tutor to help him cram for examinations? What are the chances of his buckling down to hard study, working nights and parts of holidays, of seizing every spare minute for self-betterment, self-improvement, in the same way as the boy who knows he will not have a dollar which he does not earn, who knows there is no rich father or uncle or generous friend backing him?

How can a boy develop any self-reliance or independent manliness by having somebody else do practically everything for him? It is the exercise of a faculty that makes It strong. It is the struggle to attain that brings out the stamina.

I do not believe it is possible for a man to put forth the same amount of exertion, to struggle with the same exasperation of purpose as when he feels that all outside help has been cut off; that he must stand or fall by his own exertion; that he must make his own way in the world or bear the ignominy of failure.

There is something about the situation of being thrown absolutely upon one's own resources, with no possibility of outside help, that calls out the greatest, grandest thing in a man, that brings out the last reserve of effort, just as a mighty emergency, a great fire or other catastrophe calls out powers which the victim never before dreamed he possessed. Power from somewhere has come to his relief. He feels himself a giant, doing things which were impossible for him just before the emergency. But now his life is in peril. The wrecked car in which he is imprisoned may take fire, or he may drown if he clings to the wrecked ship. Something must be done instantly; and, like the invalid mother who sees her child in peril, the power, the force, which comes only in sheer desperation, rushes to him and he feels a strength which he never before felt aiding him to escape.

Man has always remained close to the brute where he has not had to struggle to supply his necessities. Want has ever been the great developer of the race. Necessity has been the spur which has whipped man up from the Hottentot to the highest civilization. Inventors, with pinched, hungry faces of children staring them in the face, have reached into the depths of their being and laid hold of powers which wrought miracles. Oh, what has not been achieved under the pressure of want, of stern necessity! We never know what is in us until we are put to the test, until some great crisis uncovers the hidden power which lies so deep in our beings that no ordinary occasion can call it out. It responds only in emergencies, in desperation, because we do not know how to reach deep enough in the great within of ourselves to lay hold of it.

A boy once told his father he had seen a woodchuck up a tree. His father said that that was impossible, for woodchucks did not climb trees. The boy insisted that a dog got between the woodchuck and his hole and he just *had* to climb the tree. There was no other way out of it.

We do "impossible" things in life simply because we have to.

Self-reliance has been the best substitute for friends, influence, capital, a pedigree, or assistance. It has mastered more obstacles, overcome more difficulties, carried through more enterprises, perfected more inventions, than any other human quality.

The man who can stand alone, who is not afraid of difficulties, who does not hesitate before obstacles, the man who believes in his own inherent power to do things he is the man who will win.

One reason why so many people carry such little weight in the world is because they are afraid to do things or to have convictions. They do not dare to do their own thinking, or to be positive. They must trim a little here and a little there so as not to antagonize. They put out feelers to see how you stand and whether you agree with them before they dare assert what they think, and then their opinion is merely a modification of your own.

There is something in human nature which loves the genuine, the true, the man who has an opinion of his own and dares to assert it, who has a creed and dares to live it, who has convictions and dares to stand by them.

We only feel contempt for the man who does not dare to show himself, to express his opinion until he knows ours, for fear he may run counter to them or offend us. The man we respect and would imitate is he who fixes his aim beyond the range of the narrow vision of those about him, who has the courage and grit to stand forth and do his duty regardless of criticism. Such a man is not disheartened because he is not understood, for he knows that it is only the long-sighted who can see his target, that if he takes a long range his object must invariably be invisible to most of those about him.

There is a powerful tonic in holding the conviction that you are in the world for a purpose, that you are there to help, that you have a part to perform which no one else can take for you, because everyone else has his own part to fill in the great life drama. If you do not act your role, there will be something lacking, a want in the production. No one ever amounts to much until he feels this pressure that he was made to accomplish a certain thing in the world, to fit a definite part. Then life seems to take on a new meaning.

17
MENTAL FRIENDS AND FOES

We can make our minds art galleries of beauty or chambers of horror; we can furnish them with anything we please.

WE THINK in mental images.

They always precede the physical realities. The mental pictures are copied into the life, etched upon the character. The whole physical economy is constantly translating these images, these mental pictures, into life, into the character.

A thousand times better allow thieves to enter your home and steal your most valuable treasures, to rob you of money or property, than to allow the enemies of your success and happiness discordant thoughts, disease thoughts, sick thoughts, morbid thoughts, jealous thoughts to enter your mind and steal your comfort, rob you of that peace and serenity without which life is a living tomb.

Whatever you do or do not do for a living, resolve that no morbid, discordant, sick thoughts shall get access to your mind. Everything depends upon keeping your mental faculties clear and clean. Keep the holy shrine of your mind, God's temple, pure and free from all your thought enemies.

A discordant thought, a morbid mood, when once harbored, breeds more discordant thoughts and more morbid moods. The moment you harbor the one or the other it will begin to multiply a thousandfold, and grow more formidable. Do not have anything to do with discord or error, or the brood of morbid moods. They spoil everything they touch. They leave their wretched impression on everything. They rob one of hope, happiness, and efficiency. Tear down all these sable pictures from your mind, all the black images. Dispel them. They only mean mischief, failure, paralysis of ambition, and the death of hope.

We must stand 'on guard at the door of our thoughts; keep out all the enemies of our happiness and achievement. We have no real enemies except those which live in our own minds, which are generated by our own passion, prejudice, and selfishness.

We are so constituted that we must do right, we must go straight, we must be clean and pure and true and unselfish, magnanimous and charitable and loving, or we cannot be really healthy, successful, or happy. Perfect harmony of mind and body means a clean mentality.

What a tremendous amount of wear and tear, wrenching, rasping, aging friction we could prevent, if we had only been taught as children always to shut the doors of our minds to all tearing down, destructive enemy thoughts, and to hold in the mind ideas that uplift and encourage, that cheer, gladden, and refreshen, encourage and give hope! I have known instances where a fit of the "blues," depressing, gloomy, melancholy thoughts, sapped the life of more vitality and energy in a few hours than weeks of hard work would have taken out of the man.

We sometimes see the power of thought strikingly illustrated when a great sorrow or a disappointment or a heavy financial loss in a short time so changes the personal appearance of a man that his friends scarcely recognize him. The cruel thought bleaches the hair and seems to laugh demoniacally from the wrinkles it has made in the face.

What fearful havoc jealousy will make in a life within a few days or weeks. How it ruins the digestion, dries up the very source of life, whittles down the vitality, and warps the judgment. It poisons the very centers of life.

It is pitiful to see the wreckage of hopes and happiness and ambition in a life after hurricanes of passion have swept through the mental kingdom.

If the child were properly trained in the art of thinking, what an easy thing it would be for the grown person to avoid all this to bring beauty, poise, and serenity to the mind, instead of the desolation wrought by the enemy thoughts, the thieves of joy, the burglars of happiness and contentment.

Why do we learn so quickly that on the physical plane hot things burn. us, that sharp tools cut us, that bruises make us suffer, and endeavor to avoid the things which give pain and to use and enjoy the things that give pleasure and comfort, while in the mental realm we are constantly burning ourselves, gashing ourselves, poisoning our brain, our blood, our secretions with deadly, destructive thoughts? How we suffer from these thought lacerations, these mental bruises, these burnings of passion; and yet we do not learn to exclude the causes of all this suffering.

It was not intended that man should suffer, but that he should rejoice, and forever be happy, buoyant, and glad. It is the perverted thought habit that has deteriorated the race.

Everybody ought to be happier than the happiest of us. This was the Divine plan. We might as well say that the maker of the most perfect watch that was ever constructed planned for and intended' a certain amount of friction and imperfection, as that the Creator who ,I doeth all things well" intended that man should have more or less suffering.

To get rid of our thought enemies requires constant, systematic, persistent effort. We cannot accomplish anything else worthwhile without energy and determination, and how can we expect to keep the enemies of our peace and prosperity out of the mind without energetically resisting them, driving them out of consciousness, locking the door of the mind against them?

We do not seem to have any trouble in keeping personal enemies out of the home, people we dislike very much, people who injure us and lie about us; why can't we keep out of the reception rooms of the mind the enemies of our thought?

If we walk barefoot in the country we learn to avoid the sharp stones and briers which would lacerate our feet. It is not difficult to learn to avoid the thoughts which hurt us, which lacerate us and leave ugly scars, the hate thoughts, jealous, selfish thoughts, which leave us bleeding and suffering. It is not a deep problem; it is only a question of keeping out of the mind its enemies, and entertaining its friends.

Some thoughts send hope and joy, glad ness and encouragement, bounding through the whole system; others restrict, repress all hope, joy, and contentment.

Think of the possibilities for happiness, prosperity, and long life could we all keep in the mind strong, vigorous, resourceful, productive thoughts!

It is impossible to entertain the thought of discord while the mind is dwelling upon harmony; of ugliness while beauty is reflected in the mental mirror; or of sorrow while joy and gladness predominate.

Sadness and melancholy cannot outpicture themselves upon the body when good cheer, hope, and joy live in the mind.

If you persistently keep these enemy thoughts fear thoughts, anxious thoughts, disease thoughts, sick thoughts out of your mind a while, they will leave you forever; but if you entertain them, nourish them, they will keep returning for more nourishment, more encouragement. The way to do is to discourage them by dosing the door of your mind against them. Have nothing to do with them, drop them, forget them. When things have gone against you, do not say, "That is just my luck. I am always getting into trouble. I knew it would be just so. It always is." Do not pity yourself. It is a dangerous habit. It is not a very difficult art to learn to keep the mind slate clean; to erase unfortunate experiences, sad memories, recollections, memories which humiliate, pain us; to wipe them all out and keep a clean mental slate so far as the past is concerned.

You have no conception of the peace, comfort, and happiness that will come to you after vigorously making up your mind and persistently carrying out your resolution never again to have anything to do with the things which have kept you back, have crippled, cramped, strangled your efforts; the things which have pained you and made you suffer bitter pangs.

Have nothing more to do with your mistakes, short-comings. No matter how bitter they have been, blot them out, forget them, and resolve never again to harbor them.

Of course, this cannot be done by a single act of the will; but by persistency and determination and watchfulness one can gradually clear his mind o{ most of his enemies; and the best way to get unfortunate, bitter, cruel experiences out of the mind is to fill it with good things, bright, cheerful, hopeful thoughts.

Ideas, thoughts, like everything else, attract what is akin to them. The thoughts which dominate in the mind will tend to drive out their opposites. Optimism will drive out pessimism. Cheerfulness will tend to drive out despondency; hope, discouragement. Fill the mind with the sunshine of love, and all hatred and jealousy will flee. These black shadows cannot live in love's sunshine.

Persistently keep the mind filled to overflowing with good thoughts, generous, magnanimous, charitable thoughts; love thoughts, truth thoughts, health thoughts, harmony thoughts,-and all the discordant thoughts will have to go. Two opposite thoughts cannot exist in the mind at the same moment. Truth thoughts are the antidote for error; harmony for discord; and good for evil.

Most of us fail to appreciate the difference between the influence of diverse thoughts or suggestions. We all know how a cheerful, optimistic, encouraging idea gives a thrill of wellbeing, how it rejuvenates, re-creates. We feel its tingle to the tips of our fingers .. It permeates and quickens as an electric shock of joy and gladness; it brings with it fresh courage, hope, and a new lease of life.

The man who can keep his thought right can substitute hope for despair, courage for timidity, decision and firmness for hesitancy, doubt, or uncertainty. The man who can keep out the enemies of his success by filling his mind with his friend thoughts, optimistic, courageous, hopeful thoughts, has a tremendous advantage over the one who is the victim of his moods, the slave of the "blues," discouragement, doubt. He can accomplish more with five talents than the man who cannot master his moods can with ten.

The value of our life output will depend very largely upon the degree with which we can keep ourselves in harmony and keep from our minds the multitude of enemies which kill initiative and neutralize efficiency through destructive friction.

You cannot affirm too often or too vigorously the idea that you were made in the image of perfection, love, beauty, and truth, made to express these qualities and not their opposites. Say to yourself: "Every time an idea of hatred, malice, revenge, discouragement, or selfishness comes into my mind, I have done myself an injury. I have struck myself a blow that is fatal to my peace of mind, my happiness, my efficiency; all these enemy thoughts cripple my advance in life. I must destroy them immediately by neutralizing them with their opposites."

It does not matter whether it is fear, anxiety, worry, dread, *jealousy,* envy, selfishness; whatever can in any way mar the symmetry and beauty of life should be expelled as a fatal enemy.

Acute worry, anxiety, jealousy, bad temper, nasty disposition, all these things are symptoms of a diseased mind, acute or chronic. Any sort of discord or unhappiness is an evidence that there is something wrong inside of you.

The time will come when we shall realize that every fit of anger which racks and wrenches the delicate nervous system, every touch of the hatred and revenge thoughts, every vibration of selfishness and fear, .anxiety and worry even the temporary passing through the mind of a jarring or discordant thought will leave its indelible mark in the life and will mar the career.

When discordant from worry, anxiety, anger, revenge, or jealousy, you may know that these things drain your energy and waste your vitality at a fearful rate. These losses not only do no good, but grind away the delicate mental machinery, inducing premature age and shortening the life. Worry thoughts, fear thoughts, selfish thoughts are so many malignant forces within us, poisoning the blood and brain, destroying harmony and ruining efficiency, while the opposite thoughts produce just the opposite result. They soothe instead of irritate, increase efficiency, multiply mental power. Five minutes of hot temper may make such a havoc in the delicate cell life of different parts of the body that it will take weeks or months to repair the injury, or it may never be repaired. Terror, horror, a great fear shock, have many a time permanently' whitened the coloring matter in the hair, and produced permanent aging marks on the face.

When we realize, therefore, that these emotions and all forms of animal passion are debilitating, demoralizing, that they mar, scar, and make fearful havoc in the mental realm, and that their hideousness is outpictured in the body in pain and suffering, in corresponding ugliness and deformities, we shall learn to avoid them as we would avoid physical pestilence.

It was not intended that man should suffer, but rejoice and forever be happy, buoyant, jubilant, and prosperous. It is the perverted thought habit that has deteriorated the race.

All that seems discordant to us is but the absence of the divine harmony, just as darkness is not an entity in itself, but an absence of light. The time will come when discord will be lost, neutralized in harmony.

Love, charity, benevolence, kindliness, good will towards others, all arouse the noblest feelings and sentiments within us. They are life-giving, uplifting. They make for health, harmony, power. They all tend to the normal, to put us in tune with the Infinite.

If we can preserve the integrity of the mind and protect it from its enemies evil and vicious thoughts and imaginings we have solved the problem of scientific living. A well-trained mind is always able to furnish the harmonious note in any condition.

Every man builds his own world, makes his own atmosphere. He can fill it with difficulties, fears, doubts, and despair and gloom, so that the whole life will be influenced to gloom and disaster; or he can keep the atmosphere clear, transparent and sweet by dispelling every gloomy, envious, malicious thought.

Hold the enduring, the immortal thought in the mind, and all discord will disappear. When the mind is held in the creative attitude, all that is minus, all that is negative the shadows and the .discords will flee. Darkness cannot live in the presence of sunlight; discord cannot dwell with harmony. If you hold harmony persistently in the mind, discord cannot enter; if you cling to the truth, error will flee.

THE END.

Made in the USA
Middletown, DE
07 April 2019